In the Spirit of
RONALD E. McNAIR
Astronaut
–An American Hero–

To Dan, Thank you for what you do for your McNair Program!

by

Carl S. McNair

with

H. Michael Brewer

Carl S. McNair 7/11/13

Published in the United States of America by
MAP Publishing, LLC, Atlanta, Georgia.
ISBN-10 0615441513
ISBN-13 9780615441511

For book orders, author appearance inquiries and interviews, contact the Publisher by email or mail:

MAP Publishing, LLC
P. O. Box 311353
Atlanta, Georgia 31131
404-346-3262
info@mcnairachievement.com
website: www.mcnairachievement.com

Library of Congress Cataloging In Publication Data

In the Spirit of

RONALD E. McNAIR
Astronaut
–An American Hero–

by

Carl S. McNair
with
H. Michael Brewer

MAP PUBLISHING, LLC
Atlanta, Georgia.

DEDICATION

———

To Ron's wife, Cheryl, and children, Reginald and Joy;
Ron's love and spirit are forever with you.

To my wife, Mary, and daughter, Desiree';
Thank you for your love and inspiration.

To my mother, father, grandparents, and ancestors;
Your prayers, sacrifices, and examples
continue to guide my life's journey.

To our teachers and educators
who never gave up on us.

TABLE OF CONTENTS

———

Prologue

"Ten-nine-eight-seven," intoned the voice of NASA launch control in the familiar countdown ritual.

At the six-second mark, the three main engines of the Space Shuttle *Challenger* fired in a deafening, controlled explosion of unimaginable power.

"Three at one hundred," radioed Mission Commander Dick Scobee, reporting that all main engines were functioning at one hundred percent of thrust.

"Five-four-three-two-one."

The enormous shuttle rose from the pad in a bone-rattling roar of primal energy, shaking off the shackles of gravity and rising into the clear sky on a pillar of fire and a plume of vaporous exhaust.

"Lift-off!" announced the launch controller, and a wild cheer rose from the spectators assembled at Kennedy Space Center.

That day, January 28, 1986, had dawned unseasonably cold for south Florida, but the weather didn't deter thousands of enthusiastic well-wishers who gathered to cheer on the launch of the *Challenger*. Along with the throngs who arrived in person to witness the flight, millions more watched on television or kept an ear tuned to the radio. American space flights had proceeded so flawlessly for the past decade that the public had lost some of the awe that had attended the earlier flights. Nevertheless, *Challenger* Mission STS 51-L, the 25th flight of the shuttle program, had rekindled popular interest because of its ethnically diverse crew.

Seven astronauts rode in the *Challenger* that morning, and we could scarcely imagine a more diverse cross-section of America. Five men and two women represented a spectrum of races, beliefs, and backgrounds. Some were career military, others civilians. Scientists, test pilots, and even a teacher found a place in the shuttle. Representatives of Judaism, Christianity, and Buddhism were strapped in side by side. If ever our space program had mounted a mission that looked like a microcosm of American society, this was the one.

Dick Scobee was the mission commander. His story had a romantic dash of the right stuff. Originally an airplane mechanic in the Air Force, Scobee went to night school in order to qualify as a pilot. He distinguished himself in a tour of duty in Vietnam and later became a respected test pilot, logging in more than 6,500 hours of flight time and learning to handle more than fifty types of aircraft.

From his earliest days, flight had fascinated Scobee, and as a boy growing up in Washington state, he enjoyed visiting the airport to watch the planes come and go. When he learned that

NASA was accepting applications, he immediately applied: the space program was a natural extension of his passion. Believing that doing what you love is worth the risk, Scobee entered the astronaut training program and served as the pilot on his first flight on-board the *Challenger* in 1984.

Serving as pilot for the 1986 Shuttle mission was Michael Smith, a U.S. Navy commander. Like Dick Scobee, Smith was a former test pilot and had an impressive flight record in aircrafts of many designs. Having completed tours of duty aboard the *USS Kitty Hawk* and the *USS Saratoga*, his military record was impeccable. He had been awarded three air medals as well as the Navy Distinguished Flying Cross and the Vietnamese Cross of Gallantry with Silver Star. NASA selected the North Carolina native as an astronaut in 1980, in part because of his specialization in aeronautical engineering. This would be Smith's first trip into space.

Judith Resnik was one of two women on the shuttle and one of three mission specialists. Raised in a Jewish family in Akron, Ohio, Resnik showed an early aptitude for the sciences. In college, she majored initially in math, then switched to electrical engineering— a field in which she eventually earned a Ph.D. She worked in several respected positions in the private sector before being selected as an astronaut in 1978. She was among the first women recruited by NASA. In 1984 she became the second American woman in space on the maiden flight of the *Discovery* shuttle, following in the footsteps of Sally Ride. "J.R.", as Resnik liked to be called, never played up the significance of her gender. Instead, she pointed with pride to the whole corps of astronauts and the rapid progress of the U.S. space program. Her peers respected her as a no-nonsense scientist and a dedicated member of the team.

Ellison Onizuka, another mission specialist, further added to the diversity of the crew. Born in Hawaii, Onizuka was a Buddhist of Japanese-American parentage. Participation in the Air Force Reserve Officer Training Corp (AFROTC) program at the University of Colorado led to a commission in the Air Force, and from the Air Force Onizuka joined NASA in 1978. Even at NASA, Onizuka remained a member of the Air Force on detached duty. His Air Force affiliation made him an ideal candidate for the 1985 *Discovery* flight, the first fully classified Department of Defense space mission.

An avid outdoorsman, Onizuka spent his free time fishing, hunting, or playing soccer with his daughters. A fan of the space program since childhood, the thirty-nine year-old Onizuka hoped to continue making space flights as long as he was physically qualified. On the 1986 *Challenger* flight, Onizuka was in charge of deploying one of the largest communications satellites ever launched and carrying out experiments related to Halley's comet.

Gregory Jarvis was one of two crewmembers who were not official employees of the Federal government. Dubbed a payload specialist, Jarvis joined the mission on behalf of Hughes Aircraft Corporation in order to conduct experiments that could lead to improved liquid fuel systems. Jarvis had been scheduled twice for shuttle flights, but he'd been bumped both times, once by a U.S. Representative and the second time by a U.S. Senator, both of whom served as on-board observers. The third time was the charm, and Jarvis was excited about flying on the *Challenger*.

In fact, Jarvis found many things exciting. A self-described workaholic, the Michigan native loved squash, jogging, cross-country skiing, and bicycling. He also played classical guitar and took regular courses at the local community college to keep his mental edge. Just prior to the flight, he spoke publicly about his complete confidence in both the mission crew and the ground support, and expressed his gratitude at being on this flight.

The other member of the crew who was not a government employee was Christa McAuliffe, the first teacher selected to fly in space. The Teacher in Space program was initiated for two purposes: to spur public support for the space program and to interest young Americans in considering an aeronautical career. A teacher of high school social studies and American history, McAuliffe was chosen from more than 11,000 applicants. Unquestionably, McAuliffe was the most recognizable member of the crew, quickly becoming a darling of the media. The New Hampshire teacher brought enthusiasm, good humor, and a self-effacing humility that immediately endeared her to the American public. In spite of the limelight and the constant interruption of interviews, McAuliffe was well liked by her fellow crewmembers.

Her responsibilities on the flight included broadcasting fifteen-minute lessons from space that would be aired by PBS in classrooms across the country. She was thrilled to be addressing the largest classroom in human history. If she found a downside to the one-year training program, it was the time away from her family. McAuliffe confessed that she missed asking her children about their day and then kissing them good night at bedtime. Her presence on the flight ensured that teachers and students in classrooms across the nation would be watching the televised lift-off.

The remaining member of the *Challenger* crew was Mission Specialist Ronald McNair, a black physicist who came from modest beginnings in a small town in South Carolina. McNair was a man who excelled at everything he attempted to do. A natural athlete with over thirty trophies from karate competitions, he was also a jazz musician, a scientist specializing in laser technology, and an active member of his church.

McNair's first space flight was on Space Shuttle *Challenger* mission STS-41B in 1984. In that crew he was the specialist responsible for operating the maneuverable arm used to place satellites in orbit. On that mission, he became the second African -American in space and the first person ever to play a saxophone in orbit. On the current mission, McNair would launch the Spartan-Halley science platform to study Halley's comet as it hurtled past the earth. This was to be his second and final flight before he turned to a career as a college professor of physics.

All of the crewmembers on the *Challenger* that cold January morning in 1986 were highly trained and extremely gifted individuals. They were pioneers who knowingly accepted the risk of pushing into the modern frontier of outer space. They were heroes one and all, deserving the highest honor and respect. We cannot possibly calculate the sum total of the intellect, courage, dedication, and spirit contained in the *Challenger* as the mighty spacecraft rose from the launch pad and mounted into the Florida sky. Nor can we quantify the loss seventy-three seconds later when the *Challenger* exploded before the eyes of a horrified world.

Much has been written about the final *Challenger* flight. Why should I add one more book to the many titles devoted to those heroes? Because Mission Specialist Ronald McNair was my brother. I knew him as no one else did. I still love him two decades later, and I want the world to share the inspiration that Ron brought to me and everyone else he touched in life. Instead of dwelling on sadness, this book will focus on determination, accomplishment, and the remarkable possibilities inherent in each and every human being. My brother, Ron McNair, died as he lived— "hanging it over the edge."

This is his story.

CHAPTER 1

A Different World

My younger brother, Ronald Erwin McNair, was born on October 21, 1950, the second of three sons in our family. I beat Ron into this world by ten months; that was the first and the last time I would beat him at anything. I can't honestly say that in those days I knew Ron was destined to accomplish great things, but I quickly figured out that he was a notch above the rest of us. Whether he applied himself to music, sports, or school, Ron stood out from the crowd. Even so, given our humble beginnings, I'm still surprised by how far he went in life.

Like most of the black families in Lake City, South Carolina, we never had much money. In the first home I remember, we had no indoor plumbing. We later moved into a better house left vacant when our paternal grandfather died. This improved our standard of living, but we still weren't settled in a mansion. On rainy days, we covered the floor and furniture with pots and pans to catch the water dripping through the leaky roof.

One room in the house we used only for storage. We kept

a freezer in there, but we tried to avoid going in because the floor was in bad shape; years of leaking water had rotted and weakened the boards. One day when Ron was about eleven years old, he went to get something from the freezer for dinner and literally fell through the floorboards. The jagged wood gashed his knee. The cut must have been three inches long and deep enough to lay open the kneecap.

Blood gushed from the wound and my parents rushed Ron to the doctor for stitches. I vividly remember two things about that accident. The first is that Ron seemed indifferent to the pain, although I'm sure his knee must have throbbed bitterly. That was a trait Ron displayed repeatedly over the years. When he played catcher for our baseball team, he had chest protection but no face guard. More than once I saw him get hit in the head by a fast pitch, and he'd simply shrug it off. He'd pick himself up and get back behind the plate, ready for the next pitch. Once after being beamed, he invited me to rub his forehead. The tissue under the skin felt like a washboard. I thought it was terrible, but Ron only laughed about it. On another occasion, a batter lost his grip and a flying baseball bat struck Ron in the mouth and knocked out his front teeth.

As I review our childhood, it seems to me that Ron was prone to such accidents. I've sometimes wondered if God allowed Ron more pain than me because God knew he could handle it better than I could. My brother took his frequent injuries in stride. He accepted physical pain without being distracted. He was so focused on his goals and passions that he didn't have leftover energy or attention to waste on pain. I'm sure one reason he excelled in so many areas was his ability to concentrate on the matter at hand and shut out other distractions, even physical misery.

My other memory of that day when Ron fell through the floor is my brother's enthusiastic curiosity and love of knowledge.

"Look at this," he said, peeling back the flaps of skin on the injury.

He studied the inner workings of his knee with fascination and delightedly pointed out to me the muscles and ligaments he recognized in the open gash. He explained how everything fit together and what role each piece of tissue played. Ron might as well have been in front of an anatomy class lecturing on his favorite subject. That, too, was typical of my brother. He loved any opportunity to learn and he was a natural teacher. I'm sure that passion for knowledge, that eagerness to understand how things work, served him well in the years ahead when he did ground-breaking research.

Ron and I grew up with a healthy respect for hard work. Many of our family members and neighbors spent time in the fields cropping tobacco and picking cotton, beans, and cucumbers. The labor was demanding and sporadic, but cropping offered ready cash for those who could endure it. Actually, Ron and I were quite eager to get into the fields, since becoming old enough to crop was a rite of passage. Around the age of twelve or thirteen we began making a daily wage as croppers whenever we weren't in school. We'd get up early, well before sunrise, and stand at the edge of the road. That vigil signaled our willingness to work. Sooner or later some farmer would pull his rattle-trap truck to a stop beside us, lean out the window, and ask, "Y'all boys want to crop my 'bacca?"

"Yes, sir," we assured him.

"Git on then."

We'd climb into the back of the truck and head off to parts unknown. The notion sounds strange nowadays, but then we'd trustingly get into a vehicle driven by someone we didn't know and with no idea where we were headed. We didn't think going with a stranger was dangerous, and even if we'd considered the risk we wouldn't have balked. After all, at day's end a princely six dollars apiece was waiting for us!

Farmers liked to use youngsters for the first cropping of the tobacco to pick the lower leaves that grew close to the ground. The veteran croppers could pick faster than us, but they didn't like the stooping that went with gathering the lower leaves. After a few hours, I understood why they spurned such work. By midday, I felt as if someone had stuck a shape knife blade deep into my lower back. By afternoon I could scarcely stand upright.

We stooped and worked our way down row after endless row. Tobacco is a rough plant and the sandpapery leaves are hard on the hands. If we weren't careful, the thick, fat tobacco worms would sting us, or maybe they bit. I was never certain, but I knew it hurt. We also had to be on the lookout for rattlesnakes that would lie in the shade of the leaves during the high heat that sometimes exceeded 100 degrees.

We worked a long day, from around 6:30 in the morning to maybe 7:00 at night. One farmer we worked for surprised us with a wonderful lunch. His wife fried chicken, cooked greens, rice, and cornbread, and the farmer invited us to eat on his lawn. We feasted like kings and congratulated ourselves on our good fortune—until we collected our pay that evening. The farmer handed each of us a five-dollar bill. Ron and I considered the money, then exchanged uneasy glances.

Working up my courage, I said, "I thought we were going to get six dollars."

"That's right, boys," the farmer said. "Six dollars for a day's work, but I had to charge you a dollar apiece for lunch."

A whole dollar for lunch? I was angry and disgusted. If I'd known we were going to have to pay for lunch, I'd have said no thank you. I could have brought a cinnamon bun and bologna and ended up a dollar richer.

Our cropping career was an eye-opener. I discovered first-hand how hard some people had to work just to make ends meet. My mother was a schoolteacher, but she also spent summers working at the tobacco barns. She was especially adept at wrapping the leaves into bundles, securing them with tobacco twine, and then stringing the bundles onto poles to be hoisted into the barns for drying. Every step of growing, picking, and processing tobacco is demanding work and no cropper ever got rich.

Ron and I decided we'd diversify and try our hand at picking cotton, but we soon changed our minds. A few days working in the cotton patch convinced us to return to tobacco cropping. Cotton grows in a hard, spiny husk, so in no time, our hands were bleeding. We looked around and saw old women out-picking us and their hands looked fine. Either they knew a secret we never figured out or years on the job had toughened their skin. In picking cotton, the goal is to gather a hundred pounds of cotton in a day's work. Can you imagine how much light, fluffy cotton is required to weigh one hundred pounds?

Ron and I picked as fast as we could, but our sacks weren't

filling up. At some point that day we decided to combine our sacks so that maybe we'd reach the quota together. Still, our take of cotton was tiny and discouraging. As the day wore on we grew more desperate. I started throwing mason jars of water into the cotton, hoping to get it wet and increase the weight. Finally, I resorted to hiding a couple of field stones in the sack, but our deception was uncovered. Usually the foreman simply weighs each sack of cotton at the end of the day and pays the picker. I don't know if the foreman suspected us or if we simply had bad luck, but he decided to empty our sack into another. As he did so, the field rocks came thumping out.

We were busted. He looked at the pitiful pile of cotton and the rocks we'd added, and shook his head sadly.

"Y'all boys know better than that," he said.

Our career as cotton pickers was mercifully short. We never got the hang of it and soon returned to tobacco cropping. Over the next few years we spent enough time in the fields to know that we didn't want to invest the rest of our lives in tobacco cropping. The sweat-soaked days we spent picking cotton and plucking tobacco leaves gave us a powerful incentive to remain in school and prepare to make a living some better way. I am still humbled by the memory of gray-haired men and women who spent their whole lives at such labor.

In many ways our growing up years in Lake City were unexceptional. We went to school, attended church, goofed off when we could, and worked hard when we had to. Our friends, neighbors, and family members shared the same experiences that shaped us all as we matured through our teen years into young adulthood. We had a childhood typical for those raised in the rural south in the 1950s and 1960s.

On the other hand, the passage of half a century has made that era feel strange and distant by contemporary standards and values. You might think Ron's first trip to another world came when he climbed into a spacecraft in 1984 and launched into outer space. However, as I look back, I realize Ron and I grew up in a world quite different from the one I'm living in today. Television was still a novelty in 1950, the year Ron was born, and remained an extravagance in our early childhood. In fact, the first television to which we had access wasn't in our own house, but in the home of our grandparents, a huge black and white set that picked up two channels and took several minutes to warm up.

Forget about home computers, the internet, and cell phones. That was the imaginative stuff of the gaudy science-fiction stories Ron and I loved to read. We did have a phone, but it was the old-fashioned rotary dial type, and we shared a party line with neighbors down the road. When Ron and I started school in 1954, Jonas Salk's polio vaccine was not yet available to the public, nor had the world witnessed the birth of lasers, Velcro or the hula-hoop. That year, the first national broadcast of a color television program took place. Not many people noticed, since there were only two hundred color television sets in existence.

The differences between today's world and the world in which I grew up are more than technological. In many ways, our culture has changed even more radically than our scientific know-how. Not until 1954 did Thurgood Marshall bring challenges to the Supreme Court that resulted in the official ruling that segregated schools were unconstitutional. Even after desegregation became the law of the land, putting that legislation into practice took years of effort and sacrifice. My youngest brother, Eric, spent his last year of high school in an integrated school, but Ron and I never attended a desegregated public school. In both elementary and high school we were assigned to black schools and would have been forbidden to attend the better funded white schools in our community. I say "would have been" because we never considered the possibility of crossing the color line. We lived in a black and white world and we knew our place. Preachers had been run out of town for dealing with the NAACP, and I remember when a cross was burned in the front yard of Mr. Walter Scott, our scout leader. We knew that if we got "uppity," some people in town would make it their business to "straighten us out."

The black families in our little community lived on the other side of the tracks, and that wasn't just an expression in Lake City. The railroad really did run through the center of our community, and the whites lived on one side while blacks were consigned to the other. That railroad track remains a vivid symbol of the South in which Ron and I spent our formative years, its few feet of timber, steel, and gravel creating a seemingly insurmountable division between the two races. Although at the time, most of us accepted that sad arrangement as "the way things are," in the years ahead, my generation would help change America for the better. Some of us did so in dramatic ways. Others, like my brother, quietly expanded the boundaries and pursued achievements forbidden to African-Americans of earlier generations, proving that we could hold our own with America's best and smartest.

I don't want to give the impression that we grew up wallowing in self-pity. I don't recall ever feeling sorry for myself. Ron and I had a good childhood, laughing and crying, making friends, playing, and surrounded by the love of our family. I only mention the disadvantages of our youth to make a point. Many people unfairly diminish the accomplishments of someone like Ron. They say, "He was probably born with a silver spoon in his mouth. I'll bet he had life handed to him on a platter. To get so far he must have started near the top." I suppose people say such things in order to make excuses for themselves, to explain why they haven't accomplished much. So many people are afraid to dream great dreams. They are scared to take a risk or set a challenging goal. Their setbacks and obstacles are so overwhelming that they fold their arms and give up. They justify an attitude of defeatism by emphasizing their own difficulties and belittling the successes of others.

This is one reason I want to tell my brother's story to a new generation. The life of Ronald McNair proves that a tough beginning doesn't have to lead to mediocrity and disappointment. Not everyone has the same natural gifts, but we all have the power to shape our own future. Where we end up is not predetermined by where we start. Our choices, our dreams, and our determination will decide our destiny. That was true of Ron as it is true of every genuinely successful person.

CHAPTER 2

The Ties That Bind

Whatever Ron, Eric, and I lacked, at least one precious commodity blessed our childhood. Our lives were indescribably enriched by people who loved and believed in us. Our father, Carl, was a gifted, intelligent man. Dad didn't have a lot of education, but he was one of the smartest men I've ever known. He was poised and smooth, a wonderful communicator, and had a way with people. I wish I were half the public speaker he was. There was never anything "country" about him. He also loved music and sang in a gospel group, so maybe that's where Ron got his musical gifts.

By trade, Dad was an auto body repairman. For some years, he worked for local auto body shops, restoring and painting cars. Eventually, he opened his own shop. He worked hard and he was skilled and meticulous at his craft, but he never reached the level of the success he deserved in that business. No matter how hard he worked, he couldn't provide for us the way he wanted. He didn't talk much about his financial frustration, but I know it bothered him.

Our mother, Pearl, was a schoolteacher and a lifelong inspiration for us. Mom had a thirst for knowledge and a zeal for learning. She graduated from high school as class valedictorian. When I say she graduated from high school I should explain that black students only went through the eleventh grade at that time. That was as far as the courses went in black schools in our community.

I don't understand why things were set up that way. I'd hate to think that the system intentionally tried to handicap our mother and her generation from competing with whites for jobs. Did the school board assume that blacks weren't going to college and therefore didn't need as much education? Maybe eliminating the senior year from black schools was a way to save the school district a few dollars.

Regardless of the reasons, an eleven-year education didn't slow down my mother. She went to college, majored in education, and came back home to teach. Most people would have stopped with a college degree and a good job, but not Mom. She wanted to push on and earn a master's degree, but obstacles loomed in her way. With three kids at home, she couldn't afford to quit teaching. Her best option was to work full-time and go to school part-time.

That plan presented another problem—a difficulty that would have discouraged most people. No college with a graduate program was near enough to Lake City for Mom to easily commute. Mom did it the hard way. She enrolled in a graduate program at South Carolina State College in Orangeburg one hundred miles from home. Her dedication still amazes me. Three times each week she and three friends, also teachers, drove a hundred miles to class and then another hundred miles home. Of course, that commute followed a full day at work. Between her teaching, her time on the highway, her work in the master's program, and her household responsibilities Mom pioneered the practice of multi-tasking long before that expression came into vogue. Not that she complained. Mom loved school so passionately that I think she welcomed the challenge and treated the whole thing as an adventure. She kept up that grueling pace for six years before she finally earned her master's degree. The work and determination that went into that accomplishment still make me proud.

In those days, Ron and I undertook a learning project of our own. Mom was away so often, while Dad worked such long hours at the auto body shop, that we frequently had to cook our own meals. At first, we were clumsy and inept in the kitchen, but we learned enough to fill our bellies. Fending for ourselves was our contribution to Mom's continuing education. A dish made of tomatoes, rice, and sausage became a staple at our house. Like our home life, that recipe was simple and basic but hardy enough to nourish us.

As much as we learned from Mom and Dad, other people also made significant contributions to our lives. My mother's parents, Mable and James Montgomery, were the soul of our family. My brothers and I spent a lot of time in their home. When Mom commuted to class, we went to their house after school. My grandmother usually welcomed us with a pan of hot biscuits and a jar of molasses or a bottle of cane syrup. No wonder we were glad to be there. They also had a television set before we did, and we loved watching TV.

Granddaddy was a small man, and Grandmother was a short woman with gray hair. Our grandparents weren't physically imposing, but they had huge hearts and our neighbors showed them sincere respect. I didn't think of them as old because they were active, involved people. Both were leaders in local Cub Scout and Boy Scout troops.

My grandparents were every-Sunday members of Wesley United Methodist Church. Granddaddy was the church treasurer, and Ron, who was naturally good with numbers, helped count and record the offerings. Grandmother was a woman of faith and prayer. My developing faith was shaped by the heartfelt and moving prayers she used to offer as we gathered at the table. When called on to pray at church, she did so enthusiastically. When my grandmother prayed aloud we could tell she knew God first-hand; she was a personal friend of the God of Abraham, Isaac, and Jacob.

For instance, years later when Ron prepared to launch on his first shuttle flight, over a hundred friends and relatives from the Lake City community made the trek to Florida to watch the lift-off. At the space center, the NASA bus took us to the designated viewing area a couple of hours before liftoff. When the bus stopped, we were eager to get out and find a good vantage point. Grandmother sat near the front and before we could tumble off in a rush she stood, raised her hand for silence, and said, "Let us pray!"

Two years later when Ron's second shuttle flight ended in tragedy, our grandmother was too ill to make the trek to Kennedy Space Center. Even so, she anointed that mission in fervent prayer. The Bible teaches that the prayers of the righteous are powerful and effective. Of course, God has plans that are bigger than ours and doesn't give us everything we ask for.

Still, God certainly heard Grandmother's prayers. Who can

deny that her intercession made a difference to Ron in the last moments of his life? I choose to believe that her prayers back in South Carolina eased my brother's departure in the skies over Florida. On that sad day, maybe she once again prayed for a safe homecoming for Ron. If so, God surely answered that prayer.

Like many people in Lake City, my grandparents made a living by whatever they could find to do. They worked hard for little return. My grandfather once owned a small general store and worked in the local mills. Before he retired he was a foreman managing Carter's Flour Mill, one of the largest in the region. Grandmother also worked in the mills and made baskets for the bean and cucumber crops.

Grandmother was a great advocate for education. That's probably where Mom got her zeal for school.

"Y'all boys stay in school," she told us repeatedly. "And don't be cuttin' up in class. You've got a chance to make something of yourselves, but you'll never get anywhere in this world without an education. You have the good brains God gave you. You've got everything you need. The rest is up to you."

Ron and I grinned at each other whenever Grandmother launched into that speech. We heard it so often we could have finished the sentences for her. Even so, we took the lesson to heart. Perhaps my grandmother was so vehement on the subject of education because circumstances had forced her to drop out of high school. Growing up in a poor family, the need for immediate income outweighed the long-term advantages of staying in school. Like so many of that day, Grandmother traded her books for fieldwork at an early age.

After Ron and I began to earn money by cropping tobacco,

her words carried even more weight. No one needs to be ashamed of honest labor, even the lowliest work. I respect those who do what they have to do to get by in the world, but neither Ron nor I wanted to be trapped in those tobacco fields for the next sixty or seventy years.

In the area of education, 1971 was a landmark year for our family. That was the year Ron and I both graduated from college. That alone would have been cause enough for family rejoicing, but we had additional milestones to celebrate. My younger brother, Eric, graduated from high school at the same time, as did our cousin, Debra.

The Lake City High School Class of 1971 contained one more member of our family. Grandmother took her own advice to heart and went back to school. After a respite of so many years, she had to learn anew how to study. She always seemed to have a book nearby or homework assignment due shortly. She joked that both the textbook print and her brain had shrunk over the decades. The books were harder to read and the facts didn't want to stick in her head. She stayed committed even when courses were tough. Quitting doesn't run in our family. Grandmother was determined to reach her goal.

On commencement day, amidst the long procession of teenagers, was my sixty-five-year-old grandmother, who proudly marched across the stage to the accompaniment of wild cheers from friends and family. After a half-century delay, the principal handed Grandmother her hard-won and long-postponed diploma.

Ron and I were there that day along with the rest of the family. Nothing could have made us miss that event. We brought along our college mortarboards and gowns and posed with the lady of the hour. While Mom fiddled with the camera, moving a few steps forward, then backward, I whispered to Grandmother, "We're proud of you."

"I'm proud of us all," she replied. "I wish my parents could see me today."

"Maybe they can," I said.

She nodded thoughtfully.

"I wasn't sure I could do this. Things come harder when you've been out of school a long time. But if an old lady can get one of these," she said, wagging the diploma, "then anybody can—anybody who really wants it."

"What will you major in when you get to college?" Ron asked innocently.

Grandmother rolled with the joke.

"I haven't made up my mind," she said. "I've heard physics is easy."

We all laughed as Mom begged us to hold still.

"How can I get a picture with you jerking around like chickens with your heads cut off?" she asked.

One of my most treasured possessions is the family photograph showing us three brothers, my cousin, and my grandmother standing side-by-side in academic garb. In that creased color photo we are all smiling hugely, but Grandmother's expression projects an indescribable joy and sense of accomplishment.

Looking back, I can easily see the seeds that were planted in

Ron, the seeds that grew into commitment, perseverance, and a never-say-die attitude. My brother consistently set the highest possible goals for himself—some said they were impossible—and he faced many setbacks and obstacles on his way. He was strengthened and encouraged by the love of learning instilled in him from childhood. He carried in his heart the memory of our grandmother, proudly clutching her diploma at an age when many people retire from life.

Ron and I weren't the only ones blessed by Grandmother's indomitable spirit. That dear woman raised three families. My grandmother brought up her own biological children, my mother, Pearl, and her two sisters, Mary and Lela. As a parent myself, I can appreciate how much love and energy Grandmother poured into that task. The character and accomplishments of her daughters reflect her success.

Then after my mother and my aunts were on their own, my grandparents took in two more children. Their mother was unable to raise them herself when her health failed. The elaborate network of social services that we enjoy today wasn't available in those days. Rural families sometimes "adopted" orphans or children in need without the involvement of courts or formal legal proceedings. My grandparents saw a need and responded. Both of those children, Amos and Betty Lee, went on to college.

My grandparents then raised two more children, Edward and Barbara Hughes. Edward grew up to be a firefighter and member of the National Guard; Barbara earned two educational degrees and established her own accounting business.

Add to those three families my brothers and me, since my grandparents also had a hand in raising us. How Grandmother and Granddaddy could afford to feed so many mouths is beyond me. Together, they probably earned no more than thirty dollars a week. Even though money was in short supply, there was no shortage of love flowing through that household. Without fanfare or worldly success, my grandparents made a positive and lasting mark on the children who passed through their home.

A person's life is a river. The contributions of friends and family members flow into our lives like tributaries. Each positive influence strengthens us and encourages our progress. In turn, we flow into other lives downstream. We become tributaries ourselves, passing along the lessons we've learned and the love we've received.

For instance, Barbara, who became an accountant, now has a daughter who has earned a medical degree. I wonder how many other lives will be enriched in the course of her practice. People who have never heard of Grandmother or Granddaddy will reap the benefits of their faithful, humble lives.

As we gaze downstream toward generations beyond our sight, we can only imagine the ongoing heritage of my grandparents. We can neither calculate their eventual influence nor number those who will be blessed by the compassion and guidance of those two good people. God alone knows how long a single act of kindness continues to flow through the years.

My grandmother's rich life and heritage is more impressive in light of the fact that she was only one generation away from slavery. My grandmother's father, Jack Peterson, was born a slave and her mother, Mariah, was born to slave parents just after Emancipation. My family's story, like those of so many others, is testimony to the strength of the human spirit.

Even though I'm part of that story, I can hardly believe that only a few decades separate the birth of my great-grandfather into slavery and my brother's participation in America's conquest of outer space.

How could my family have moved so quickly from impoverished bondage to aerospace adventure? Part of the answer lies in the greatness of this country. America has made her share of mistakes and will make more, but at the heart of this nation is a dream of freedom and a longing for all her sons and daughters to have the opportunity to become the best we can be. We have moved toward the fulfillment of that dream slowly and sometimes painfully, but we have made progress. That journey from slave ship to spaceship in four generations would not have been possible in any other nation in the world.

However, America is made not only of ideals but also of people. The history of our nation usually focuses on our famous sons and daughters—the statesmen, the generals, and the politicians. I don't want to minimize the achievements of such great leaders, but we must also acknowledge the contributions of those whose names are overlooked in the history books. This nation was built through determined effort, and by the hard work and great sacrifices of unnoticed working people like my parents and my grandparents.

I love my brother Ron and I hope future generations remember his story, but I also know that the accomplishments of Ronald McNair would have been impossible without the love, support, and guidance of the quiet and unassuming people who went before us and blazed the path.

CHAPTER 3

Showdown at the Library

Although I was ten months older than Ron, we enrolled in school at the same time thanks to my father pulling a bit of chicanery. In our town, some students started in the first grade at the age of five. When the time came for me to begin school, Ron was only four years old. My brother was already showing signs of the brilliance he would later exhibit in the classroom, and Dad felt he should begin his formal education. Why hold him back a year if he was ready to start? Dad was certain our local school, Carver Elementary, wouldn't accept Ron. We were well known in the community, and everyone realized Ron was underage.

My father came up with a plan to bypass that problem. He took Ron to a school a few miles away in the country at Camerontown. A friend of my mother's served as principal there, and the scrutiny was less intense in that tiny rural school. Dad enrolled Ron by telling the teacher that he was five years old, and Ron was so bright that no one questioned the deception. My brother easily kept up with the other students in his class. So Ron and I went through first grade at the same time in two different schools.

By the beginning of the next school year, Ron was five years old and Carver formally admitted him and allowed him to enter the second grade. From that time on, my little brother and I were in the same public schools, the same grade, and in most of the same classes.

The local black schools didn't get the same funding as the white schools. In subjects as diverse as music and chemistry, our teachers improvised lessons to compensate for the absence of supplies and resources. We never had the pleasure of fresh, new textbooks. Our books were grubby and marked up with loose pages and broken binding because they were the worn-out discards from Lake City Elementary or Lake City High. When the white students considered their books unusable, the school district kindly passed the texts along to us.

In spite of the disadvantages, we black students received an outstanding education. We were blessed to have truly excellent teachers. In those days African-Americans had few opportunities to put their education to work. The white-collar jobs generally open to black people were preaching and teaching. Our school administrators were able to hire the brightest and most gifted educators from the black community. A surprisingly high percentage of the teachers under whom Ron and I studied had been valedictorians and salutatorians. We got the cream of the crop, and we knew it. Every day we experienced the dedication of our teachers, their devotion to us, and their make-do creativity in class.

In 1954 the Supreme Court ruled that segregated schools were separate, but not truly equal. That was true in terms of books, libraries, equipment, and buildings. But our teachers at Carver were first-rate. They cared about us and expected us to do our best. In fact, they insisted on it.

Mr. P. C. Lemmon, our principal, often told us, "Never settle for 'That'll do.' A little extra effort will make your work even better."

From our first day in school the teachers hammered into us that as black students we had to try twice as hard, work twice as diligently, and learn twice as much to make our way in the world. Nothing would be handed to us; we'd have to earn it with intelligence and hard work. Because the teachers buoyed us with their high hopes, we gave them our best. The heart of any school is its faculty, and we had the best. Neither Ron nor I were embarrassed by the education we received in public schools.

Ron loved school and he did well in every subject. He was consistently at the top of the class. He expected to be there and everyone else expected the same of him. Ron really inspired the rest of us to try harder. We wanted to beat him, and even when we couldn't, we wanted to close the gap between us. We thought, "Even if I can't get a one hundred percent score like Ron, maybe I can get a ninety-nine percent".

My brother brought two driving passions to his schoolwork. First, he wanted to understand everything he got involved with. In any subject, Ron wanted to know how it all fit together, why things connected as they did, and how it worked.

Second, Ron burned with an insatiable curiosity. He asked

an endless stream of questions in class, sometimes questions the teachers had difficulty answering. Even if the teachers sometimes tired of my brother's questions, they appreciated his lively mind that unearthed exceptions to the rules and sought for connections between subjects.

One day in physics class in high school, my brother challenged the teacher's solution to a problem. In this case our teacher, Mr. Norman Bartelle, was in over his head. He was actually a math teacher who had been asked by the school principal to teach a physics class.

Irritated by Ron's challenge, the teacher held out a piece of chalk. "Ronald, maybe you think you can do a better job."

I slumped in my desk and silently prayed, "Ron, don't do it. Just this once, please shut up and sit back down. You're going to get in trouble."

My prayer went unanswered. Ron walked to the blackboard, took the chalk, and worked the problem without hesitation and without mistakes. To Mr. Bartelle's credit, he didn't hold a grudge over the embarrassing confrontation. Instead, he graciously admitted his limits and enlisted Ron's help for the remainder of the course.

Ron's curiosity sometimes led to trouble. During our junior year in high school, he and I took chemistry. I found it to be a tough class, but not him. As usual, he was frustrated that the teacher was moving through the material too slowly, or so it seemed to him. Nobody else felt we moved too slowly. Sometimes, I thought we were going much too fast. On this occasion Ron decided to quicken the learning curve and further his understanding of chemical reactions with an extracurricular experiment.

Ron and our friend, Archie Alford, sneaked into the chemistry lab while our teacher, Mr. Norris Brown, was out of the room. They "borrowed" a fist-sized piece of sodium. My brother knew that sodium would react with water, and he wanted to see exactly what would happen when the two came together. Ron didn't know what he was doing, but at least he had the good sense to perform the experiment outdoors. A small crowd gathered to watch while Ron filled a galvanized tub with water.

"You're sure you know what you're doing?" Archie asked under his breath.

"More or less," Ron said. "We'll get a reaction when the sodium makes contact with the water."

"What kind of reaction?"

Ron flashed a confident smile.

"You'll see," he said.

My brother held the sodium at arm's length. After a few heartbeats he let it fall into the tub. A tiny piece would have been enough, but he dropped in the whole chunk.

Ron wanted something dramatic and he got his wish. The sodium sizzled in the water for a few seconds and then exploded. The sudden eruption splashed water on onlookers and pelted the crowd with bits of sodium. Ron's co-conspirator Archie danced a frantic jig, brushing wildly at his sodium-plastered hair. We were lucky that no one lost an eye and nothing caught on fire.

If Ron had been a different kind of person, that accident

might have brought his science career to a premature end. Instead, the fiasco fired Ron's enthusiasm for chemistry and deepened his curiosity about the way in which different compounds react with one another. The kid who almost blew up his schoolmates with a piece of filched sodium would later do some of the earliest research on chemical lasers at MIT.

If curiosity was one of Ron's passions, the other was competition. He liked being number one in class. If I saw a correction on Ron's paper or a less-than-perfect score on a test, I could count on my brother lingering after class to learn from his mistakes.

"What did I leave out of this essay?" Ron would ask, laying an A-minus paper on the teacher's desk.

"Where did I go wrong in this problem, and how can I fix it? Did I use the wrong equation or make a mistake in my calculations?"

"What should I do differently to make sure I get an "A" next time?"

School wasn't the only arena where Ron's competitive spirit burned brightly. A local radio show also energized his passion for winning. As we got ready for school in the mornings we listened to a call-in program that featured a daily trivia question. The subject might be politics, science, history, but South Carolina history was a favorite topic. The radio announcer would throw out a question and challenge the listeners to call in with the answer.

Ron, Eric, and I loved that show. We worked out a system for calling in. Thanks to Mom's love for learning, our home contained more books than the typical Lake City household.

Dad had even bought us a set of encyclopedias. So two of us would position ourselves to look up the answer to the question, and the third brother sat by the phone to make the call. Of course, in those days we didn't have speed dial phones; however, we discovered we could dial all but the last digit of the radio station phone number and have our telephone primed for the call. As soon as we had the answer, we had only to dial one last digit and the call would go through.

For all this effort, glory was our only reward. We didn't win money, products, or groceries. All we got out of it was the thrill of winning and the excitement of hearing our names on the radio.

When the disc jockey announced, "Congratulations to the McNair boys. They've done it again," we clapped and cheered as if we'd earned a gold medal at the Olympics.

"Those McNair brothers," Ron shouted, " are the 'baddest' boys in town."

We weren't the only family competing for public recognition. Somewhere in Lake City the Kelly brothers were also trying to call in. Oddly, we never knew who the Kelly brothers were, even in such a small town as ours. We only knew they were out there trying to rob us of our rightful fame.

After declaring our victory, sometimes the announcer added, "I wonder where the Kelly brothers are today."

After conquering the Kelly brothers, my brothers and I exploded in a victory dance.

"Those Kelly's must have overslept today," I jeered.

"Nah, their alarm went off," Ron gloated, "but they were afraid to get out of bed."

"Afraid of us," Eric chimed in. "Scared of the McNair brothers!"

We didn't keep a strict count, but we McNair boys were convinced our total wins outnumbered those of our rivals. At least that's how I remember it. Of course, the Kelly brothers might tell a different story.

That sort of contest appealed to Ron. Throughout his life, whatever he took on, he tried to be the best. Sometimes he competed with others; most times he competed with himself. If he felt he could have done better, getting the highest score on a test wasn't good enough for my brother. As Ron matured, more and more he pitted himself against himself. He looked at what he had accomplished so far, and said, "I can do better and go farther than I have before!" Competition was not simply about beating someone else; the goal was to improve his own performance, to become the best he could be. He always aimed for excellence. Competition was a tool he used to move himself closer to the achievement of his goal.

Not that Ron's competitiveness always found healthy outlets. He and I experienced the typical sibling rivalry between brothers. Perhaps ours was more intense than usual because we were close in age and the younger brother often surpassed the older. As the first-born, I felt that I should be in the lead, but Ron was such a bright person he assumed he should be in front. This led to an ongoing competition between us in almost every area of our lives.

Ron and I loved each other deeply. Because we were so close, most of the time our rivalry was good-natured. In some ways we were more like twins than just brothers. My parents even dressed us alike.

Sometimes, however, we fought like bitter enemies. Of course, boys always fight with each other, but Ron had a temper that made things worse. Any little thing might unexpectedly set him off. Without warning a wrong word or a disagreement could ignite a burning rage.

One day Ron came after me with a baseball bat. He didn't strike me, but he brandished the bat as I cowered in the corner of the living room.

"Just say one word," he screamed at me. "Go ahead. Shoot your mouth off and see what happens."

His expression was an ugly mask of rage. He trembled as he stood over me, shaking the bat a few inches from my face. Whatever we quarreled about was so trivial I have long since forgotten it. Quivering in the corner, I kept my mouth shut and waited for the storm to pass. I want to believe my beloved brother wouldn't have hit me with the bat, but at that moment I truly feared him.

I don't want to give the wrong impression of Ron. In general he was easygoing and likeable. We shared wonderful childhood years, playing, exploring, and adventuring side-by-side. He was everything I wanted in a brother and a best friend. But anger lurked below the surface.

I've never been able to explain that anger to my own satisfaction. Maybe my brother recognized his potential early and chafed at the limited opportunities in his young life. I suppose growing up black in the South in the 1950s and 1960s played a part. Ron recognized more clearly than I the disadvantages we were struggling against.

Many years later, I read the story of Dr. Ben Carson, another gifted African-American who grew up in impoverished circumstances in the inner city. He also struggled with nearly uncontrollable anger. Taming that anger changed the course of his life, allowing him to become one of the country's most gifted surgeons.[1]

I hate to think what might have become of my brother Ron if his temper had gone unchecked. As he grew older his outbursts became less frequent and volcanic. Perhaps that was simply a natural sign of maturity, but I think Ron made a conscious decision to establish control over his emotions. His anger became a source of energy.

My brother intentionally funneled his temper into healthy channels and used that inner power to fuel his later accomplishments. In a football game, on a karate mat, or even in a tough homework assignment Ron focused his seething feelings into productivity and achievement. Anger never fit well with who Ron was. In spite of his occasional eruptions, I remember him as a person whose character was essentially kind, considerate, and cheerful. I'm thankful he mastered his rage, instead of allowing the anger to overpower his life.

The best of Ron's personality shone in one remarkable event that took place when my brother was nine years old. He decided he needed some books from the Lake City Public Library, but in 1959, the public library wasn't truly public; it existed only for the convenience of the white community. We understood the unwritten rule that excluded blacks from the library, just as we were excluded from other facets of public life. We sat in the balcony in the movie theater, drank from the

"For Colored Only" water fountains, and knew better than to join the white customers at the counter in the local diner. That was the world we lived in and we accepted it.

At least, most of us did.

Ron wanted books, so he went to the library. He ignored the glares that followed him as he wandered among the shelves. Disgusted patrons shook their heads, but nobody made a move to eject my brother. A nine year-old black boy was a nuisance, but not sufficiently threatening to elicit action—at least not yet.

After some browsing, Ron chose two books he wanted to check-out of the library — an advanced science book — the other, a calculus book. Even as precocious as he was, I'm sure my nine-year-old brother wasn't ready for calculus. I doubt if he understood it, but he was determined to take them home.

Ron carried the books to a table. In block letters he carefully printed his name on the card for each volume. Then he carried the books to the front desk and waited his turn. The stares aimed in my brother's direction grew more hostile.

Ron clutched his books and gazed straight ahead. When he reached the counter, the frowning librarian took his books and studied them suspiciously. She set the books on a table behind her and said, "You can't check these out. The books here are not for colored people."

She lifted her pinched face to the person standing in line behind Ron, but my brother didn't budge.

"I want those books, please," he said.

"He couldn't possibly understand those books," she told the

library at large. "One of them is a calculus book."

The library patrons laughed, even those who didn't know what calculus was.

"You shouldn't be in here," the librarian said to Ron. "You need to leave the library."

Ron shook his head.

"Right now," she added more forcefully.

"This is a library," Ron said. "I want to check out these books."

"I don't know if he can read or not," an elderly man offered, "but he sure as hell can't hear." The patrons laughed again.

The librarian reached over Ron's head, took a stack of novels from the person behind him, charged them out, and handed them back. My brother held his position in front of the desk and forced the librarian to work around him until no one else was left in line. The stern librarian glowered down at him, and he met her gaze steadily. Practically everyone in the library had abandoned their books, newspapers, and magazines to watch the showdown.

"Can I have my books now?" Ron asked.

"Give him the books," a matronly woman called. "What's the harm?"

For a few more minutes the table remained intact, the librarian trying vainly to intimidate my little brother with the stare that normally cowed unruly visitors into apologetic silence. Ron stood patiently before the desk, looking up at her with wide, dark eyes.

"Very well," the librarian told the room in clipped syllables. "I know how to handle this."

She lifted the phone receiver, consulted a list of numbers on her desk pad, and dialed the police station.

"I'm calling from the public library," she said. "We have a disturbance here. Could you please send an officer as quickly as possible?"

She broke the connection, smiled sweetly at Ron, and then dialed the operator.

"Could you connect me to the McNair house? Pearl McNair. Thank you."

After a pause, the librarian identified herself and said, "Pearl, your boy is over here at the library causing a ruckus. He wants to check out books, and you know I can't do that. I've tried to be nice about it, but he won't cooperate. As a courtesy I'm calling to let you know the police are on their way. It's out of my hands now. I think you'd better get over here."

She dropped the receiver into the cradle with the air of a woman who had gotten the final word. She looked at Ron again, a smug smile stretching her hatchet face.

"Boy, by the time this is over, you won't be able to sit down for a week," she told him. "If you're not in jail."

In response, Ron turned his back on her and hoisted his butt onto the counter.

"I'm getting tired," he said. "I'll sit while I wait."

The police arrived a few minutes later. Two officers stalked into the library looking for trouble and found a skinny fifth-grader seated on the front desk, sneakered feet dangling, waiting patiently.

"What's the problem?" the taller officer asked.

"This boy won't leave," the librarian explained.

"I want my books," Ron told the police.

"And he's not going to get them," the librarian snapped.

The other officer, shorter and heavier, asked her, "What do you want us to do?"

"Remove him from the library," she commanded.

The officers exchanged uncertain glances. The taller policeman stooped to Ron's eye-level. "Son, why don't you just run along home?"

"Soon as I get my books," Ron said.

"He's not causing any trouble," the heavy policeman said. He surveyed the room, noting the expectant faces turned in his direction.

"And he's just a kid," the taller one added. "This doesn't look like police business to me."

"Me neither," said the other officer, wiping a sheen of sweat from his forehead with one thick index finger. He dried the finger on his shirtsleeve. "Maybe it'd be easier if you just let him have the books."

The librarian stiffened like a flagpole. Enunciating each word with elaborate precision, she said, "We don't circulate books to Negroes."

At that moment my mother hurtled through the library doors like a lioness determined to throw herself between danger and her cubs. She took in the policemen and the librarian with a quick glance, and then stepped up close to my brother.

"Ronald, what are you doing?" she asked quietly.

He nodded at the books lying on the table behind the counter. "I'm gonna check out those books," he said.

The librarian began, "Pearl, I already expl—"

"Why can't I have them?" Ron interrupted. "I'll take care of them."

"And if he doesn't, I'll pay for them," Mom said.

The librarian looked to the police for support, but they avoided her eyes.

"I don't see anybody breaking the law," the heavy-set officer muttered to his partner. To the librarian he added, "Ma'am, what do you figure is the easiest way to settle this so we can all get on with our business?"

In sullen silence, the librarian opened the books. She stamped the due date on the slip of paper glued on the last page of each book. Then she closed the books, stacked them, and handed both to my mother. Mom handed the books to Ron.

"What do you say?" she prompted him.

"Thank you ma'am," he told the librarian.

With the precious books under one arm, Ron slipped from the counter and landed lightly on the tile floor. As he and Mom left the library, every gaze followed them through the door.

Outside on the library steps, Ron didn't shout or dance a victory jig. He'd just wanted the books, and he'd been prepared to wait as long as necessary. His moral triumph was accidental and unplanned. Nonetheless, from that day forward, my little brother checked out whatever books he wanted, and the Lake City Public Library became a little more public.

Historians make note of the date February 1, 1960, when four African-American students from North Carolina Agricultural and Technical College in Greensboro crossed the color line and sat down at a Woolworth's lunch counter. The waiter refused to serve them; in turn, they refused to leave. That day marked a dramatic turning point in the struggle for civil rights and popularized the strategy called the "sit-in." Most people don't realize that a few months earlier little Ronald McNair enacted his own sit-in for the sake of liberating two books from the library.

Now you know the rest of the story!

---

¹ Ben Carson with Cecil Murphey, *Gifted Hands* (Grand Rapids, Michigan: Zondervan Publishing House).

CHAPTER 4

Challenges and Stepping Stones

Ron was no bookworm. He didn't fit the cartoon stereotype of the nerdy genius: a tiny kid with thick glasses, always carrying a huge stack of books under his arm, talking in long sentences with big words, studying every waking minute, and never emerging from his room except for meals. Except for the glasses, none of that applied to my brother. He was a normal kid, having fun, getting into trouble, and interested in a hundred different things.

For instance, Ron and I were both Boy Scouts. We loved going to Scout camp and meeting other boys from all over the state. Ron joined gleefully in the fun-filled Scout activities. We laughed about Mr. Fred Bell, our camp director, who held our spending money for us in the camp's bank. Once a day he'd ring a bell and, like a town crier, he'd shout, "Bank open!"

He also rang the bell for mealtimes, and all the scouts sang crazy songs before digging into the food. Standing side-by-side at the table, Ron and I sang at the top of our lungs, "Here we stand like birds in the wilderness, birds in the wilderness, birds in the wilderness. Here we stand like birds in the wilderness waiting for the food to be served!" We were fortunate to learn to swim at Scout camp since the pools in Lake City weren't open to blacks. Ron pressed on in the Boy Scouts and later became a Star Scout. Like so many boys before and after us, we learned responsibility and good citizenship from our participation in the Boy Scouts. Along the way we had a lot of fun.

Ron and I also played in the school band. Music was one of the rare instances when I led the way and he followed. I decided to play clarinet in the band because I thought it looked like an easy instrument to play. Was I ever wrong! In the usual spirit of friendly rivalry, Ron also joined the band. He couldn't stand the thought that I might get ahead of him on something. He also took up the clarinet but soon switched to the saxophone. He made music as if he'd been born for it.

"Ron, you've got what it takes," Mr. Edward Cooper, our band teacher, said. "I think you should pursue music. You have a natural talent for it."

Ron remained noncommittal. I don't think he ever seriously entertained the notion of music as a professional calling. But from those high school days he carried on a life-long love affair with the saxophone in particular, and jazz in general.

In later years, he carried his sax with him whenever he traveled. I recall once a flight attendant balked at allowing Ron to carry his sax onto the plane with him. My brother was calm, but adamant.

"My saxophone stays with me. If it doesn't fly with me on this plane," he said, "neither do I."

The airline relented, and both Ron and his beloved sax

made the flight together. Later the two of them would make a much higher flight together—on board the Space Shuttle *Challenger*.

For a person of such strict discipline and scientific training, the saxophone offered my brother a way to get in touch with his emotions and share them with the world. Ron called jazz a very creative kind of artwork.

"A jazz musician," he said, "is able to project his feelings through the instrument and is able to express himself creatively. That's what I enjoy about it."

Football was the next challenge Ron took on. In the ninth grade he tried out for the team. True to form, I couldn't stay behind, so I joined the team, too. Admittedly, Ron and I were not likely candidates for the bruising high contact sport of football. Neither of us were big boys. I weighed in at about 126 pounds soaking wet. Ron was a little bigger than me, but I doubt if he tipped the scales at more than 135 pounds.

The assistant coach, Mr. Robert Byrd, was tough on all of us and me in particular. I think he was trying to make me quit because of my small size. Coach Byrd put me up against one of my teammates who must have weighed over 300 pounds. Maybe my memory exaggerates his size, but he was huge compared to me. This 'giant' blocked me so hard, I just toppled over backwards. Once I was off my feet, he fell on top of me, smothering my ability to move! If we backed off from rough contact, the coach would make us run laps around the field.

I remember one day I got tired of hitting the ground. I couldn't stand any more physical punishment. I purposely dodged my adversary just so I could do the laps. Running around the field was a relief and rest period compared to getting crushed by a monster twice my size.

Ron, however, loved the contact of tackling in football. The bigger his opponent, the more eagerly he rose to the challenge. The physical contact thrilled him. He played what was called halfback in those days and also defensive linebacker. He enjoyed the linebacker position because it allowed him to hit people, and hit them he did. I once asked our new head coach, Jack Williams, why he wouldn't allow me to play defense. He just shook his head and said, "Somebody might step on you."

Ron and I were on the same team, but when it came to football, he was by far the better player. The coach once called Ron a "vicious" player, but he smiled when he said it, and he meant it as a compliment. By this time, Ron had outgrown his hot temper, but I wondered if the football field offered my brother a way to dispel his anger in a healthy and harmless way.

Both Ron and I learned to push ourselves beyond our limits on the football team. We had a charging dummy set on a sled. In practice we'd hit the dummy over and over, driving the sled backward. Our assistant coach, Mr. Byrd, was a very large man. He liked to climb on top of the sled and have us push him up and down the field.

He'd yell, "Ready! Set! Hut!" and on signal we'd smash into the charging dummy while he weighed it down.

The first few times we hit the dummy weren't too bad, but the drill continued long after we were exhausted.

"Now's the time!" Mr. Byrd shouted as we wore down. "Now's the time! Short, chocky steps!"

I never did figure out what chocky steps were, but his

challenge motivated us to keep trying. We found more
strength, we pushed harder, and finally we'd be on the far side
of the field with this heavy tackle dummy ridden by Mr. Byrd.
Ron and I carried away the same valuable lesson from our
football days. When you are down to your last breath and you
cannot take another step, that's the time to suck it in and push
a little harder. With determination and short steps you can
go farther than you dreamed. All of us are capable of more
than we realize. The achievers and the champions are ordinary
people who try a little harder and push a few steps farther. An
additional ounce of sweat, an extra dose of determination, five
more minutes of effort—that's the difference between winners
and wannabes.

When Coach Williams took over the team he had trouble
keeping Ron's and my name straight on the football field, so
he began calling us The Gizmo Brothers. I was called Little
Gizmo and Ron, bigger and taller than me, became Big Gizmo.
Names like that tend to stick, so we remained the Gizmo
brothers until we graduated.

Even though he wasn't good with names, we loved Coach
Williams. He taught and brought something new to our
team: respect! Instead of just sending us out to knock people
down and move the ball as best we could, he created workable
plays and made sure we had the blocking we needed. Coach
Williams scraped up the money from somewhere to get us
new uniforms. We couldn't afford new shoes, too, but Coach
took our old shoes and painted them gold, one of our school
colors. No knight in armor ever took more pride in his finery
than we did in those new uniforms. We actually had two
jerseys apiece, one white with blue numbers and one blue with
gold numbers. For the first time we ran onto the field feeling

like we were somebodies instead of nobodies.

We'd never gotten recognition before, but when Coach rewarded us with lettered football jackets our team pride and spirit were taken to a new high, on and off the field. That bold "C" stitched on our jackets declared us to be athletes and leaders of the school.

Coach Williams taped our ankles before each game. One by one he knelt before each boy, taking his time to carefully wrap each player's ankle. Sometime love shows up in unexpected ways. With Coach, the taping ritual proved his love for us. Taping our ankles was no odious chore to finish as quickly as possible. Coach meticulously wrapped the tape tightly enough to keep our ankles firm, but not so tightly that our feet tingled from bad circulation.

"How does that feel?" he'd ask. "Gotta take care of those ankles. Don't want anybody getting hurt if we can help it."

Tape was expensive and our athletic program was on a shoestring budget, but Coach never scrimped on the tape. In spite of the cost, he wrapped layer after layer around our ankles. We were more important to Coach than a few bucks worth of tape. Our safety and our comfort mattered because Coach cared about us. We all recognized that tape as a sign of caring.

Although we didn't bring home any championship trophies, we finished that season respectably. We felt like champions anyway, thanks to Coach. Even when we lost he made us feel like winners. He awarded individual and team effort trophies. He even filmed one of our last games. The cost of developing the film was so expensive that we never got to see ourselves on the screen, but the gesture touched us. Coach Williams made us feel important and we loved him for it. We'd have done anything for that man.

Ron excelled at football as he did at most things. He was named Most Valuable Player and he deserved it, but he had gotten something more precious than a trophy from his football years. Ron said that football taught him to never give up, no matter how tough things become. As he pushed on through life in difficult classes and demanding circumstances, quitting was never an option. The challenge of football was a steppingstone into the future.

Ron played other sports as well. He was as naturally gifted on the athletic field as in the classroom. He ran track, and he ran without me. I wasn't too motivated to run unless someone was chasing me. However, track appealed to Ron's sense of self-competition. He was always trying to improve his time, to shave a second or two off his personal best. He played baseball, too. Not only was Ron an impressive athlete, he was a natural leader as well. At one time or another my brother was the captain of the track team, the baseball team, and the football team.

He was also a leader off the field. Although he could cut up and play jokes with the best of us, he was the sort of person others looked up to. Personal conduct was one facet of his leadership. He was considerate and fair to other people. His religious faith was genuine. He never used vulgarity and rough language. He would have nothing to do with drugs. He set his own high standards, and he held himself to them. When decisions had to be made, friends usually asked his opinion. He consistently tried to do the right thing, even when that was the hard thing.

One of the toughest challenges for Ron and me came when our parents separated. When Ron and I were ten and eleven years old, respectively, our father moved out of the house and went to New York. Dad had grown so frustrated by his inability to make decent money in Lake City that he was desperate to make a change in his life. That he couldn't give us all the things he wanted us to have was a continual disappointment for my father. He went to New York with the hope of making things better for us all. In the beginning, I think Dad had every intention of returning home, but that never happened. He came for visits, but we never lived together again as a family. My parents didn't formally divorce, but they lived in different parts of the country and our home was broken. Eric was so young that I'm not sure how Dad's departure affected him, but speaking for Ron's and my hearts were broken.

Not that Dad dropped out of our lives. He tried hard to stay in touch and to be the best father he could from a distance. He faithfully sent money to support the family, and he came home for holidays bearing gifts that were extravagant by our standards. Even after we got into college, Dad still bought us suits and Polaroid cameras, hoping to make up for not being around.

As youngsters we visited Dad in New York as often as we could. Whenever we could catch a ride or Dad could afford to pay our way on the Greyhound, we trekked off to New York carrying our "greasy bags" of home cooking to feed us on the way. We spent most summers with Dad in whatever apartment or boarding house he was living in at the time. He helped us find work in New York, and we came home in the fall with money in our pockets. Even when we were underage, we still found jobs. Pretending that our birth certificates had burned in a house fire, Dad would vouch for our age and we'd go to work for whoever would hire us. We weren't proud of our deception, but it beat working in those hot tobacco and cotton fields.

To be fair about it, Mom and Dad got along better when they weren't living together. Dad made every effort to remain in our lives while we grew up, but things just weren't the same. We missed having him at home with us. Boys need a father and ours was far away. He wasn't there for Scout meetings or band concerts. In my modest football career I only once caught a touchdown pass, and I wish Dad had been there to cheer me on and slap me on the back after the game.

We weren't desolate, of course. Granddaddy was a welcome and steady male presence in our lives. We were also blessed with men we admired in church and at school, men like Coach Williams and Mr. Cooper, our band director, who meant so much to us. Still, Dad's absence was painful for Ron and me, the great grief of our childhood.

That experience of separation taught both of us the importance of family ties. While he lived, Ron was a devoted father to his children Reginald (Reggie) and Joy. He loved playing with them, and squeezed in as much time with them as possible. He often took them along to NASA or Karate Class just to show them off. In the same spirit, I've tried to be a father who's always there for my daughter, Desiree.

Ron did great things in his too-short life, but I know he'd agree that family comes first. Without people to love and people who love you, our accomplishments mean very little. Even in this brave new world of the space age, love matters most.

CHAPTER 5

———

The Space Race

Ronald McNair came into this world while our nation was struggling to get out of this world. In the days following World War II, many German rocket scientists came to work in the United States space program. At first, most rocket research was carried out at White Sands, New Mexico, but in 1950, the year Ron was born, Cape Canaveral launched its first "bumper rocket," a two-stage rocket equipped with a secondary thrust that kicked in after the craft reached the upper atmosphere. The bumper rocket was an important step in space flight. The double-thrust system paved the way for today's multi-stage rockets in which lower stages help to lift the rocket and then fall away to make room for the second stage engine to continue raising the now-lighter craft.

America had fired bumper rockets in White Sands, but from the date of the first launch in Florida, Cape Canaveral assumed greater importance in the American space program, soon becoming the heart and nerve center of aerospace technology.

Throughout the 1950s, Russia led the way in the space race and America maintained a disappointing second place. In 1955 President Eisenhower committed the US to placing an artificial satellite into orbit around the earth as part of the International Geophysical Year, to be celebrated in 1957-1958. Following through on the promise proved harder than anyone anticipated.

The Russians beat us to the punch again. In fact, we weren't even a close second. On October 4, 1957, the Soviet Union officially ushered in the Space Age with the successful launch of *Sputnik*, the first man-made satellite. Less than a month later, the Soviets scored a second victory when they launched *Sputnik 2*, carrying the first space traveler. The cosmonaut, as the Russians dubbed their space travelers, happened to be a dog named Laika, but the world gasped in awe at the accomplishment nontheless.

If a dog could orbit the earth safely, it was only a matter of time before humans followed the canine pioneer into space. A month after Laika went into orbit, the US attempted to send our own satellite into space, but the Vanguard rocket carrying the satellite exploded on the launch pad. Fourteen months later America succeeded in launching *Explorer 1* into orbit, but the Soviet Union was unquestionably winning the space race.

One Russian coup followed another. In 1959 the Soviet space program launched three lunar probes, one of which succeeded in photographing the mysterious dark side of the moon. The following year, two more Russian canine cosmonauts rocketed into orbit, and, unlike the unfortunate Laika, these dogs returned to earth safely. Strelka and Belka became global celebrities overnight. They were the first earthlings to reach space and return again to *terra firma*—and they weren't Americans.

In 1961, Russian cosmonaut Yuri Gagarin became the first human being to reach outer space. He orbited earth only once and his flight lasted a mere 108 minutes, but human history achieved a new milestone that April day. Ten months later, Alan Shepard followed in Gagarin's figurative footsteps and symbolically brought America into space. For the first time since the world began, the human race had shaken off the chains of gravity and truly taken the first step beyond the confines of our ancestral home. If we could orbit earth, then we could leave earth altogether and launch ourselves into the vast universe. The moon was the logical next step, then the planets, and then— Who knows? The sky was no longer the limit for human aspiration. The explorer's spirit that had taken humankind to the remotest corners of the earth now reached for an immensely grander horizon, an infinite frontier limited only by our courage and our technology.

The American public fell in love with the aerospace program. Each step forward was a topic for discussion and celebration. Astronauts were the heroes of my generation—brave, committed, and romantic pioneers pushing the boundaries of human knowledge. We studied the space program in school and talked about it at the dinner table. Space fever struck Ron with particular ferocity. Although barely seven years old at the time, my brother was thrilled by the successful launch of the first *Sputnik*. He worked the satellite into every conversation. Ron's friends grew tired of his continuing fascination with *Sputnik*, but his enthusiasm never waned. In the years that followed I would sometimes see Ron lying on his back in the grass, simply staring into the sky. From the faraway expression in his eyes I could tell he was in another world, pondering the mysteries of outer space and the possibilities of traveling there.

When there wasn't fresh news from NASA, Ron further stretched his imagination by reading science-fiction stories, a popular literature that came into its own in those days. Behind the eye-popping covers of tentacled monsters and ray-gun toting spacemen, many science-fiction writers demonstrated their own training in science and made surprisingly accurate predictions about future technology. I'm sure Ron enjoyed the bizarre stories, as his passion grew toward a career in science.

Unfortunately, fear and anxiety lurked just beneath the surface of America's space-mania. After all our efforts and accomplishments, the Soviet Union continued to lead the way into space. America was accustomed to leading and being in the forefront; the Russian achievements rankled our pride. In fact, we feared the Soviet Union's success in space. Our uneasy alliance during the dark days of World War II had chilled into Cold War antipathy by the 1950s. We distrusted Communism and felt we had to be on constant guard against the Russian threat. Hadn't Communist leaders promised to bury America?

The space race constituted a major component of the Cold War competition of those days. Neither nation wanted to be upstaged by the other in the world arena. The conquest of outer space also beckoned to both sides with the lure of military superiority. Some believed that if the Russians were the first to conquer space, they would be in a position to also conquer the earth. America hadn't forgotten the devastating rain of Nazi V-2 missiles on England in World War II. Those rockets gave Germany an edge that nearly broke the Allied resistance. Who knew what would happen if the Soviets established a foothold in space, perhaps targeting America with orbiting weapons?

I leave it to the historians and the political scientists to decide whether our national fear was prudence or paranoia. I know that it was real at the time, and our concerns about Communism both fueled our eagerness to reach space and disturbed us with every Soviet advance. When Congress established NASA—the National Aeronautics and Space Administration—in 1958, America entered the space race in earnest, both for the sake of scientific progress and also to improve our footing in the Cold War.

President John F. Kennedy stood before Congress in 1961 and made what may be his most famous speech. Less than six weeks after cosmonaut Yuri Gagarin had circled the globe, President Kennedy threw down the gauntlet and challenged our nation to land a man on the moon and return him safely to Earth. His challenge included a timeline. America would accomplish this monumental undertaking before the end of the decade.

From that point, the international competition accelerated, although the Soviet Union remained a few months ahead of our best efforts. On February 3, 1966, the Russian spacecraft *Luna 9* completed a quarter-million mile voyage across the gulf of space and became the first spacecraft to accomplish a soft landing on the surface of the moon. The world watched in awe as *Luna 9* transmitted photos of the stark lunar surface. Among other things, the landing of *Luna 9* allayed concerns that the surface of the moon might not be firm enough to support the weight of a space vessel. In June of that same year

America safely landed our first lunar visitor, *Surveyor 1*.

Exactly fourteen weeks after the arrival of *Surveyor 1*, another space age event occurred of which serious historians have taken little notice. The date of this event, more likely to turn up in trivia books than reference books, signaled a turning point for Ron. That fall my brother and I encountered a vision of the future that would shape Ron's destiny. As odd as it may sound, I'm referring to the debut of a prime-time television drama. On September 8, 1966, the first episode of *Star Trek* aired on NBC.

Even science-fiction fan, Ron had never seen anything like this. Gene Roddenberry's weekly chronicle of the *Starship Enterprise* was a wildly imaginative and ground-breaking program "beamed into" the homes of space-obsessed Americans. Once Ron and I got a taste of this, we never missed an episode. "*StarTrek* night" was the highlight of the week. In those days before home video recording technology, television fans planned the day's activities around favorite programs. We made it a point to settle in front of the screen a few minutes before the stroke of the hour. After all, the TV set had to warm up before the picture appeared, and we didn't want to miss a second of the action.

In retrospect those *Star Trek* episodes appear crude by today's standards, but we weren't tuning in for the acting or the special effects. *Star Trek* appealed to us because the story was truly visionary. Here was science raised to the nth degree. Computers talked. Spaceships traveled faster than light. Medical instruments accomplished miracles of non-invasive surgery and healing bordering on magic. Alien civilizations met and interacted. Human beings "transported" through space, their molecules disassembled at Point A and instantly reassembled at Point B.

I thought Gene Roddenberry and his writers were making up all that stuff. That was fine with me. I enjoyed the intergalactic ride, but Ron was already searching for the science behind the fiction. *Star Trek* stretched his notions of what might be possible someday and gave him the opportunity to play with the notions of theoretical physics.

Of course, Ron was way ahead of me in that department. Only many years later, during a visit to the United States Space Foundation conference, did I realize that *Star Trek's* wonders were extensions of scientific principles. During that visit I heard NASA scientists and engineers discussing black holes, wormholes, and the possibilities of matter-antimatter propulsion. To hear real scientists and engineers treating *Star Trek* seriously shocked me, but Ron knew all along.

Even more than the scientific extrapolations, Gene Roddenberry's optimistic vision of future society captivated Ron and me. The bridge of the *Starship Enterprise* was the microcosm of a healthy and egalitarian society where all sorts of people worked together in mutual respect.

The engineer was a miracle-working Scotsman nicknamed Scotty who could repair, improvise, and/or jimmy rig any piece of equipment—just in time. Mr. Sulu was the helmsman, a Japanese-Filipino given the daunting responsibility of steering the great starcraft. He was also the weapons officer in charge of firing the phasers and photon torpedoes. In the second season, Roddenberry added a Russian to the bridge, Ensign Pavel Chekov, the navigator. In our own living room we were treated to the sight of a Russian, our mortal enemy, working alongside other star-travelers in peace and good will.

The most fascinating character on *Star Trek* was unquestionably Mr. Spock, the science officer whose half-human, half-Vulcan heritage was a not-too-subtle parable on the possibilities of cooperation and love across racial lines. His alien philosophy of "Infinite diversity in infinite combinations" was a thrilling dream of what our nation and our world might someday become if people of different races and cultures could only learn acceptance and cooperation.

For all the intriguing personalities on the *Enterprise*, it was Lt. Uhura who captured our hearts. Uhura, a beautiful black woman, was a citizen of the Bantu Nation of United Africa. She was also communications officer for the ship. As a black woman she had two strikes against her in our twentieth-century world, but in the enlightened society of the twenty-third century she was a high-ranking and fully capable starship officer. The lovely Uhura saw the crew through more than one crisis with her impressive knowledge and cool head. In her off-duty time she dressed in traditional African garb, taking pride in her heritage. Even her name was a sign of black pride: Uhura is Swahili for "peace."

Ron and I fell in love with Lt. Uhura, and we weren't the only ones. The fictional Uhura was played by Nichelle Nichols, an able actress who was also a gifted singer and dancer. To see such a positive black role model on primetime television thrilled Ron and me, as well as our friends. Black actors in lead roles were still a rarity on television. Only one year before had Bill Cosby broken new ground with his starring role in *I Spy*.

Can a mere television show actually change attitudes and ambitions? *Star Trek* certainly deepened Ron's interest in science and aerospace exploration. Gene Roddenberry's weekly glimpse of the future offered similar inspiration to many others. For instance, Dr. Mae Jemison, the first African-American woman in space, has unapologetically admitted that watching Lt. Uhura awakened in her the dream of someday becoming an astronaut. Years later, in a gesture of appreciation, Mae Jemison always opened her duty shift on the shuttle with the same words: "Hailing frequencies open!" The line, of course, was Uhura's most famous piece of dialogue as the communications officer for the *USS Enterprise*.

Even NASA was smitten with Nichelle Nichols. The Space Agency hired the actress to serve as an ambassador of goodwill to assist in recruiting more women and minorities into the aerospace program. In that role she visited colleges around the country and encouraged people of both genders and all races to consider bringing their gifts to America's newest frontier.

Ironically, in *Star Trek's* early days, Nichols almost left the show. Disappointed in how little time her character received on the screen, she had made up her mind to look for a better job elsewhere. When Dr. Martin Luther King, Jr. heard of her decision, he urged her to reconsider. In the struggle for equal rights, Dr. King felt that the highly visible presence of an African-American woman in such a popular program spoke volumes about the dreams to which black people were aspiring. Nichols heeded his advice; and later, her place on the show became more prominent.

Prior to starting his career as an astronaut in 1978, Ron met Nichelle Nichols in person. At the time he was living in California. After NASA had accepted him into the astronaut training program, his friends, Dianne and Keith Quarles, threw a party to celebrate. Ron invited me to the party, but I was still in Boston finishing up my final semester in graduate school at Babson College. I was reluctant to take time away from preparing for crucial final exams and research projects that would determine whether I would graduate, so I begged off.

Had I known that Nichelle Nichols would be there, I would have made Ron's party and perhaps delayed my graduation: Nichelle Nichols was worth it. I've since regretted not attending the soiree, but I'm glad Ron got a chance to chat with the person who meant so much to us as children, as we leaned toward the television set and absorbed new ideas about the world. As far as celebrities are concerned, Ron wasn't the sort to be star-struck, but this was, after all, Lt. Uhura, and we were both *Star Trek*-struck.

CHAPTER 6

———

Ten Years Hence

Ron and I spent our summers as most school kids do. We savored the time off from school and enjoyed the rich possibilities of bright, sunny days. Ron and I played baseball, he was a star catcher; I was a respectable left fielder. Along with as much goofing off and recreation as we could cram into three fleeting months, we also looked for work. We usually spent part of the summer in New York with Dad, enjoying his company and taking advantage of job opportunities there.

In other words, the long summer days were hardly long enough to contain everything we wanted to do. No one was more surprised than I when Ron decided to spend a precious summer in school. I liked school as much as the next person, but most students didn't willingly go to school during the summer when they didn't have to. Sometime my brother's behavior mystified me. Early in our junior year in high school, Ron impressed our chemistry teacher, Mr. Norris Brown, by his quick grasp of the subject and also by his consistent hard work. After observing my brother for a few months, the teacher had taken him aside for a private conversation.

"Ronald, have you ever heard of the Summer Science Institute?" Mr. Brown inquired. He explained that each summer some of the brightest science students from around the southern states gathered at Virginia Union University in Richmond.

"What do they do there?" Ron asked.

Mr. Brown told him that for two months the students conducted experiments, performed science research, heard lectures, and took part in intensive, first-class science learning experiences.

"How does that sound to you, Ron?" Mr. Brown probed.

"How much does it cost?" Ron wondered.

"Well, Ron, all of your expenses would be covered. There'd be no cost to your family for you to attend the Summer Science Institute," assured Mr. Brown.

"I'll need some time to think about it," Ron said.

I figured he was trying to think of a way to get out of going to the Science Institute without hurting his teacher's feelings. I was wrong. Ron wanted to go, but he was uneasy about being away from home for such a long time. Life in a small town has many advantages, but it doesn't open your eyes to the possibilities of the big, wide world. Ron and I had made many trips to New York to visit Dad, but that was different from attending the Science Institute. When we got off the bus in New York we had family waiting for us. Besides, we rode the bus together. Ron had never traveled alone, and he didn't know anyone in Richmond, Virginia. In our view of things, that was a long, long way from home. What if Ron got to Virginia Union and he didn't like it? Or, he ran into trouble?

Or, he became homesick? He'd be on his own with no family nearby to help.

I wonder if Ron also worried about being able to keep up with the other bright students. At Carver High, he was a big fish in a small pond and he was used to being number one in every class. At Virginia Union, all the students would be above average, and Ron might find it much harder to excel. Yet, to think of meeting other students from all over the South sounded very intriguing.

After deliberating and soul-searching, he made up his mind to apply for the Summer Science Institute. Did he decide the trip wouldn't be too hard or the classes too demanding? Not necessarily. In spite of his trepidation, he loved a challenge and was simply unable to retreat from a hard task. The more difficult the trial, the more he itched for a chance to prove himself. If Ron could make a running start and jump across a six-foot creek without falling in, instead of basking in glory, he'd go looking for someplace where the creek bed was seven feet wide so he could beat his own record.

The Summer Science Institute enlarged and excited Ron more than anyone anticipated. For the first time, he found himself utterly immersed in science and math. He was in class with peers who shared his passion, and he was immensely energized by the interaction with other students. Studying alongside like-minded people multiplied his level of enthusiasm ten-fold. Back home in Lake City, Ron was constantly badgering the teachers to go faster, but the teachers held back so the rest of the class wouldn't be left behind. At Virginia Union, Ron found his niche, and he never had time to become bored or wish the teacher would cover more material or move at a faster pace.

The Summer Science Institute teachers themselves were outstanding. We were accustomed to bright, dedicated instructors at Carver High, but the leaders of the Summer Science Institute were chosen especially for their teaching gifts as well as their expertise in the subject matter. Ron found no need to "help" the Science Institute teachers cover the material as he had done in physics class back home. These teachers also had a fatter budget for materials, and the lessons were never tedious or makeshift.

If *Star Trek* had helped Ron envision the bright promise of the far future, his experience at the Institute opened his eyes to the possibilities of the present and revealed to him the existence of a world much larger than he had suspected.

Apparently, my brother stood out even among the bright students at the Science Institute. One day a university professor asked him, "Have you ever considered pursuing a Ph.D.?"

Ron had never heard of a Ph.D. He admitted he didn't have any idea what that meant.

"A Ph.D. is a doctor of philosophy degree," the professor told him. "A doctorate represents the loftiest level of academic achievement. A Ph.D. is the highest degree in education."

As my brother pondered that, the professor added, "I think you are an excellent candidate for such a degree, Ronald. I'm sure you can go far if you are willing to work hard and apply yourself."

That conversation literally changed the course of Ron's life. The challenge of a Ph.D. grabbed him by the collar and wouldn't let go. If a doctorate was hard, he'd prove he was smart enough to earn one. If only the very best students achieved the doctoral degree, he was determined to go for it. At the beginning of that day, my brother had no idea that the Ph.D. even existed in academia. By the time he climbed into bed that night, he had decided to confront the challenge. The kid from Lake City, South Carolina would earn a Ph.D. He would someday be Dr. Ronald McNair.

When Ron returned from the Science Institute, most of us didn't know what to make of this latest ambition. My brother announced his decision to seek a Ph.D. and the members of our family nodded their encouragement, but some of them wondered what a Ph.D. might be. My grandfather pondered those initials, determined to make sense of his grandson's lofty goal. Granddaddy knew the Ph.D. must be something truly worth pursuing, something of great value. After considerable thought, he unlocked the secret, at least to his own satisfaction. One day he confided to me that he'd finally figured what a Ph.D. was.

"So what is it, Granddaddy?" I asked him. "What does Ph.D. stand for?"

My grandfather smiled and nodded his head knowingly.

"A Professional Hunting Dog," he told me. "That's the only thing that makes sense. No wonder Ron wants one so bad. A first-rate huntin' dog is hard to come by."

As I reflect on Ron's trip to the Summer Science Institute and his determination to become a doctor of philosophy, I realize that key people played a major role in that decision. For instance, what if our chemistry teacher at Carver hadn't recognized Ron's potential? Or, even having seen my brother's talents, what if the teacher had failed to encourage him to take a risk and try something new in Richmond? Ron would have missed out on a life-changing summer, and perhaps, he might never have realized his potential to achieve a doctorate degree.

At the Science Institute, what if a certain university professor had been too busy to initiate a personal conversation with my brother? What if he had never broached the subject of a Ph.D., never expressed his confidence that Ron was a likely candidate for that rigorous course of study? Maybe Ron's enthusiasm would have waned without an identifiable goal toward which to direct his effort. For all I know, my brother might have settled for something far beneath his ability. Throughout Ron's life, the right people seem to have arrived at the right times.

I refuse to believe that we float through the world like jellyfish bumping into random events. I am quite certain that God is at work in our lives, and provides what we need at key moments. You'll never convince me that coincidence moved Ron's chemistry teacher or that happenstance prompted that all-important conversation at the Summer Science Institute. I know He had a hand in those things. God had plans for Ron, just as He has plans for each of us. We may not all have the same gifts and talents as Ronald McNair, but we have not been overlooked either. The Creator plants possibilities in us and then provides opportunities for us to realize our potential.

To my brother's credit, whenever opportunity was presented, he was ready to listen. Whenever a door opened, Ron had the courage to walk through that door and see what waited on the other side. Life is a partnership. God blesses us with gifts and talents and helps us find opportunities to put them to work. For our part, we must hone our gifts and talents and use them to the best of our abilities. Regardless of Ron's intelligence, he wouldn't have gotten very far without hard work, risk, and courage. When we do our part, amazing things can happen.

Back in Carver High School the year after the Summer Science Institute, Mr. Brown assigned an essay to be titled "Ten Years Hence." The teacher hoped that the essay would encourage planning and goal-setting among the students. We were in our junior year and the time had arrived for us to make decisions about what would come after high school. Would we look for work? Should we go to college? If so, what would be our field of study?

Ron used the essay as an opportunity to sketch out his new ambition.

"Ten years hence," he declared, "I will have a Ph.D. in physics."

I admired Ron for going out on a limb like that. Sharing plans with his family was one thing, but going public was another. To put his aspirations into writing and to announce those plans to the school took real courage. Now he had publicly exposed his dream. More than that, he'd even proclaimed an area of study and committed to a timetable for achieving his Ph.D.

One reason why so many dreams never come true is our reluctance to make a plan and then commit ourselves to concrete goals. Relishing a fantasy is easier than wrestling a dream into reality. As long as we pretend that we'll start achieving our aspirations "one of these days," we have no pressure to succeed, and no risk of failing. We can literally spend a lifetime explaining, "I'm not quite ready. The time isn't right. I don't have everything I need yet. I'll start as soon as my life settles down and I don't have so many balls in the air." Half the tombstones in the cemetery should read: "He never brought his dreams to life."

Sometimes the fear of failing keeps us from setting a goal and struggling to fulfill it. Everybody fails sometimes, even talented people like Ron, but achievers pick themselves up, learn from their mistakes, and make a new plan. If we miss our personal deadline, we can always set up a new timetable. The only true failures in life are the people terrified of trying. People who set goals don't always reach them; people who never set goals never reach them.

In the story of Alice in Wonderland, a bewildered Alice approaches a fork in the road and has no idea which way to turn. The Cheshire Cat is lounging nearby and Alice asks his advice.

"Excuse me," she says to the cat. "Can you tell me which fork in the road I should follow?"

The cat studies Alice for a moment.

"Where do you want to go?" the cat asks.

"I don't really know," Alice admits. "I don't have a destination in mind."

"In that case," the cat assures her, "you can follow either fork. If you don't know where you're going, it doesn't matter which direction you take."

When we're going nowhere in particular, one road is as good as another, and the path of least resistance will serve us well enough. Life is easier when we settle for daydreams. As soon as we declare a goal, we're forced to plan and work to accomplish that objective. From that point on our decisions matter, and every fork in the road either takes us closer to our goal or leads us away from the fulfillment of our dream.

The one absolutely essential step toward success is the first step. On the day that Ron handed in the essay describing his plans "Ten Years Hence," he took the first step on a path that would lead him to the stars. Following that path would require single-minded devotion, hard work, and sacrifice. That path wouldn't be easy, but at least Ron had committed himself to a goal.

CHAPTER 7

——

You're Good Enough

In 1967, Ron and I graduated from Carver High School. I was proud to achieve eighth place in grade point standing, but my brother outdid me as usual. Ron's grade point average put him in first place, and he became valedictorian for the Carver High School Class of '67. In spite of our sibling rivalry—or because of it—we headed off to college together a few months later.

Aunt Lela (Austin) was our high school guidance counselor. She assisted students like Joe Wilson and Toney Graham with their college applications and they were awarded scholarships. Joe went on to become South Carolina's first black Deputy Attorney General as well as a minister. Toney became a medical doctor and pastor of a church. Naturally, Aunt Lela would help Ron and me in obtaining financial assistance, too.

We discovered that the state of South Carolina would pay out-of-state fees for black students if the state's black colleges did not offer their major in its curriculum. Ron and I qualified, and received grants to pay our out-of-state fees for four years.

We were most grateful to South Carolina. After the state schools were integrated, this practice was discontinued.

That fall we enrolled at North Carolina Agricultural and Technical State University. I was thankful to have Ron at my side as we left home and moved into a new world. I know he felt the same way.

When Mom took us to A & T's campus, we were dressed in coat and tie at her insistence. Once we arrived at our residence hall, we quickly shed those suits. Nobody else was wearing a tie, and we were happy to change into our jeans and t-shirts.

The day Mom dropped us off, Ron and I wandered around the school soaking up the sights, basking in our freedom, and feeling intimidated by the "huge" campus. By the standards of Lake City and Carver High, A & T was large, impressive, and daunting.

North Carolina A & T is a historically black college, and we had no trouble finding our way among other African-American students. We quickly made friends in our dormitory, Scott Hall, and across the campus. I pledged the Omega Psi Phi Fraternity the spring of our sophomore year. I got there first, but Ron soon followed me into Omega Psi Phi, and I sponsored his membership the next fall. Those were good years. We grew in many ways and learned enough to prepare ourselves for a place in the world.

Although we easily adjusted socially, establishing ourselves academically turned out to be harder than either of us expected. Although we received a wonderful education at Carver High, it had not entirely prepared us for A & T's rigorous math and science placement test. That first year, I suppose, I was simply majoring in college, but Ron immediately declared himself a physics major. The physics department gathered all the physics majors for an orientation and get-acquainted session.

Ron's heart sank as he chatted with students from New York, Chicago, and D.C. The big city schools had offered a much better grounding in physics and these students were far ahead of Ron. They reminisced casually about high school physic courses in thermodynamics, classical mechanics, and modern physics.

"I'm not even in the running," he told me. "These guys had so many advance physics courses in high school, I don't even stand a chance competing with them. I haven't had any of those classes. I don't even have a clue what those classes are about."

"You'll catch up," I told him nervously.

 "I don't think so. I'll bet none of those guys had to help their teacher teach a high school physics class, either," Ron said as his doubts elevated.

" What are you going to do?" I asked.

Ron shrugged his shoulders....

Prior to this encounter, I'd never seen even a hint of intimidation in Ron when faced with a challenge. His uneasiness made me very apprehensive. If Ron was having self-doubts about his academic readiness, I was in big trouble.

Barely one week at North Carolina A & T, Ron was already woefully behind his classmates. This wasn't what my brother, nor I had counted on. He was accustomed to being the top student, the guy sitting in the front desk asking questions nobody else understood, and urging the teacher to move faster. Suddenly the valedictorian was a remedial student, and he didn't like it. In Ron's eyes, the students from northern cities—that part of the country we called "up the road"—were thoroughly knowledgeable and confident. Self-doubt seized my brother. Sure he'd done well in our little high school in Lake City, but was he good enough for college physics? Maybe his trip to the Summer Science Institute had been a fluke. That university professor and those teachers in Richmond didn't really know Ron. Just because they thought he had the makings of a scientist didn't prove anything. They could be wrong.

Ron convinced himself that he couldn't possibly hold his own in class with those big-city students. I guess Ron's doubt was contagious. Before long I found myself checking the bus schedule for a one-way ticket home. If my brother, Carver High's valedictorian, couldn't hack it in college, then I didn't have a prayer. Only my loyalty to him kept me at A & T those first few months. I couldn't bring myself to leave Ron behind. I hung around to see how things would turn out. I figured if worse came to worst, we'd both flunk out and return home together—in failure.

Ron dropped out of his physics major and switched to music as his area of concentration. Of course, music is a wonderful field and requires genuine talent and dedication. No one could fault him for pursuing music. He was very comfortable with music and majoring in physics posed a serious threat to his comfort zone. Yet a career in music didn't seem the best use of his abilities. Ron was in retreat. He was backing away from his great dream of becoming a scientist. I recalled the confidence he expressed in "Ten Years Hence" and wondered if he would later regret this decision. A decade later, would he look back and wish he had given physics his best effort?

I wasn't the only one to question Ron's decision. His college counselor and advisor was a very kind and wise woman named Mrs. Ruth Gore. After my brother had been a music major for a couple of weeks, Mrs. Gore sent for him and sat him down for a heart-to-heart conversation.

"Ronald, why have you abandoned your major in physics?" she asked him.

"I like music," Ron said.

"So do I," Mrs. Gore said. "But you came here to study physics. What has changed your mind?"

"I went to a small-town high school," he said, lowering his head. "Many of the physics students here at A & T graduated from some top college preparatory high schools from big cities up North. I don't think I can compete with these guys. I'm in over my head. I don't know why I ever thought I could major in physics. I'm so far behind, I don't know if I'll ever catch up."

When he finished pouring out his heart, Mrs. Gore said, "Before you make up your mind, Ronald, would you be willing to take some aptitude tests? The results of those exams would help us understand your natural abilities and skills."

Ron agreed to the tests and a few days later he sat again in Mrs. Gore's office as she reviewed his test results. She looked at the score sheets spread upon her desk. After a few minutes she looked at Ron then returned to studying the scores. She looked at him again, back at the scores, and then Ron and Mrs. Gore's eyes met for a moment. The next words that came out of her mouth marked another turning point in my brother's young life. What she said was simple and straightforward, but her statement made a permanent mark on Ron, as if she tattooed a lasting message on his heart.

"Ronald," she said, "I think you should try physics because I believe you're good enough."

Ron drank up those words as if he were a thirsty man who had stumbled upon an oasis in the desert of doubt.

"You are good enough."

Mrs. Gore put her finger on the central matter. Ron had begun to doubt his own adequacy, but this counselor saw the insecure freshman more clearly than he saw himself at that moment. His confidence had crumbled, so she offered her own.

"You are good enough."

Once again God sent the right person at just the right time. Mrs. Gore's encouragement was all the incentive Ron needed. He switched his major back to physics and committed himself to doing his best. If Mrs. Gore believed in him, he'd take the risk of believing in himself.

A proverb says, "Anxiety weighs down the human heart, but a good word cheers it up." Ron didn't need anyone to nurse him through his classes. Once he put his mind to the task, he was able to master the requirements for a degree in physics. What he *did* need in those first weeks was a good word, a caring gesture of encouragement. He needed someone to believe in him and tell him he was good enough to accomplish whatever he set out to do.

Had Ron lived a longer life, I know he would have committed himself to becoming a mentor for economically disadvantaged students who need to hear a good word to relieve their anxious doubts. What he received from Mrs. Gore, he was eager to pass along to others. Ron had a teacher's heart. Whenever he got the opportunity to teach and inspire others he jumped at the chance, whether in a karate dojo, before a classroom, or from a speaker's podium. He'd planned to retire from the Astronaut Corps and begin a career as a college professor after his second and final flight aboard the Space Shuttle *Challenger*.

One reason Ron wanted to help others along the way was became of the assistance he had received on his own personal journey. At juncture after critical juncture, my brother encountered teachers, professors, and advisors who built his confidence and challenged him to push on in spite of his uncertainties. Having received so much support, he loved to pass on encouragement to others whenever the opportunity presented itself. Oftentimes one word of encouragement, one positive sentence, can completely change the direction of one's life. We need people in our lives who love and care about us to believe in us during those low points in life when it's difficult to believe in ourselves.

Both Ron and I took remedial courses in mathematics and science during our first year at A & T. We were disappointed to be spending so much energy simply catching up with our classmates, but our only alternative was to surrender and return home. To be honest, our freshman year was a struggle, but we hung in there. Just as Ron's initial doubts had undermined my confidence, now his determination kept me hitting the books a little harder. Although Ron hadn't entered A & T on a level playing field, by the end of our sophomore year his grades were outstanding and he was on par with his peers in the physics program.

Ron believed that God was using his accomplishments as a key to open another door of opportunity. One of his physics advisors, Dr. Donald Edwards, informed him about a program that allowed promising physics students to take summer physics classes and conduct science research at Duke University in Durham, North Carolina. Ron questioned his readiness and his ability. Duke was a prestigious and highly respected university. At Duke, he would encounter an entirely new situation. So far in his life, Ron had attended only all-black school systems. Duke was a southern university with a predominantly white student body and my brother wondered if he would fit in. This was still the age of the Civil Rights movement and black students' presence on Duke's campus was still a novelty. He also questioned whether he could keep up academically with the white students at such a demanding university.

After considerable soul-searching, Ron refused to give in to his fears. Gradually, my brother was getting the hang of confronting challenges and sailing into unknown waters. He pumped up his courage and set off for Duke University that summer. His initial worries turned out to be well founded. Duke was a tough school and at first he barely kept up. To compensate for the demanding work load, Ron worked harder than the other students, read more books, and spent more time studying. The extra effort paid off well that summer and Ron brought home grades of which he was proud.

Sometimes when I ponder Ron's life, I picture him climbing a long stairway. Each step was higher and harder than the one before. I know he was sometimes tempted to sit down and stop climbing. That next step could appear so daunting! Yet all the steps behind him, the challenges already faced, prepared him for the next one. When he stepped out on faith and attended the Summer Science Institute in Richmond, he found he was able to learn beside other bright students from across the South. Then at A & T, he discovered that he could match students from the big high schools up North. At Duke, he was tested again. That time he learned that he could compete with top scholars from across the country, both black and white students.

Ron could have called a halt at any time. He could have said, "This is far enough. I've climbed higher than I ever expected, and I'm not going any farther. That next step is too tough, and I've reached my limits." But Ron's renewed and reinforced confidence denied quitting as a consideration. Each step gave him a bigger perspective on life and higher expectations for himself. When others survey my brother's accomplishments, they marvel that he reached outer space. I was there at his side for most of the trip. I know what others may have overlooked: Ron didn't fly to the stars— he climbed there one step at a time.

In 1968, Dr. Paul E. Gray, then associate provost, and later, president of the Massachusetts Institute of Technology (MIT), chaired The Task Force on Educational Opportunity. The Taskforce was comprised of both faculty and students. Their charge was to hammer out policies and approaches that would become the basis for recruiting, admitting, retaining, and graduating African-American undergraduates and graduate students.

In 1970, another upward step loomed before Ron when another physics advisor, Dr. Thomas Sandin, offered him a spot in an exchange program at MIT. If accepted in the program, Ron would spend the spring semester and the summer at the Institute.

"The Massachusetts Institute of Technology," Ron said, speaking the name reverently. "MIT is one of the most prestigious universities in the world!"

"There's nothing wrong with A & T," I said.

"Of course not," Ron agreed. "A & T is a great school, and I'm proud to be here. But I was told that only the best students from around the world get into MIT."

Ron's voice betrayed both his excitement and his awe. To say that he might participate in an exchange program with MIT is misleading. MIT didn't send students to A & T. In fact, A & T sent a few students to MIT, and in return the Institute sent a professor to A & T to help enrich the physics curriculum and course offerings.

Once again Ron agonized over the decision. This step felt especially steep and high. MIT's reputation and mystique thoroughly intimidated him and he wrestled with misgivings.

"MIT is the cream of the crop," Ron told me. "There are no second-stringers there. Even the janitors at MIT have master's degrees."

"You're joking," I said.

"Some do," he insisted. "Instead of dispensing soft drinks and candy bars, the vending machines at MIT sell slide rules."

During his inner struggle, Ron drew on the words Mrs. Ruth Gore had spoken to him a few years earlier. "You're good enough. Go try!" With those words echoing in his head and his heart, Ron went to MIT.

There among the giants, Ron had a rude awakening. Usually our fears of the future are far worse than the reality that awaits us. As it turned out, MIT was much harder than Ron had imagined. Dr. Michael Feld, Ron's MIT advisor, said that my brother was clearly unprepared for the "MIT experience." Ron was a disciplined person and he worked hard at his studies, but he was shocked to discover that the average MIT student labors sixty or seventy hours per week on course and laboratory work.

Maybe Ron had some reservation about his decision to attend MIT, but once there he immersed himself in the heavy workload. Dr. Shirley A. Jackson, a physics doctoral candidate at the time, served as his mentor during the exchange program. Shirley later became the first African-American woman to earn a doctorate at MIT. She also became the first African-American president of Rensselaer Polytechnic Institute (RPI).

Shirley regularly invited study groups to her apartment. The students spread through the apartment, staking out turf in the living room and kitchen to study various topics. As the evening wore on, one student after another would pack up and depart for home and bed. After the other students had all left, Ron would still be there, reading intently and jotting notes. Occasionally Shirley would emerge from her bedroom, her own studies finished, only to find my brother still at work. At that, Shirley returned to her room and resumed her studies. She wasn't about to be out-done by an undergrad. Without realizing it, Ron had become an encourager for his mentor.

Ron returned from the MIT experience thoroughly

battered by the level of work expected there. Nonetheless, MIT attracted him. I've already commented on my brother's high tolerance for pain and discomfort. As the baseball injuries and the gash in his knee proved, he could endure hardship without complaint. The strenuous classes at MIT left my brother bloodied, but with head unbowed. Once he convinced himself to accept a challenge Ron always rose to the occasion. When he found himself surrounded by brilliant students, he compensated by working even harder.

When Ron and I returned to A & T the next fall, he reaffirmed his commitment to obtain a Ph.D. in physics.

"And I'm going to do it at MIT," he said nonchalantly.

"That place almost killed you," I protested.

"Pretty close," he admitted.

I was amazed that he planned to return to a school where the work had almost knocked him down for the count.

"I don't get it. Why go back to MIT?" I asked him.

"Because it's a great school," he said.

I shook my head in bewilderment.

"And," he added, smiling, "because it's also the toughest."

CHAPTER 8

———

Lunar Landings and The Riots

My brother was no cloistered bookworm. Alongside his academic efforts, Ron cultivated a well-rounded life. He found time for fun, maintained his interest in music and athletics, and actively participated in a local church, St. Paul AME. I'm amazed he found time for his many interests, but Ron consistently nurtured a number of passions simultaneously.

He readily made friends and maintained a circle of support through the diverse people he befriended at school, and among other physics students. He also established lasting relationships with professors and instructors. Through those friendships Ron showed his depths to others who were in position to challenge and guide him. His stints at Duke and MIT came about in part because of faculty members who knew him well, appreciated his potential, and were able to recommend him for advancement.

Ron kept his skills sharp on the saxophone. In fact, he joined a jazz band at North Carolina A & T. He loved jazz because it combined order and improvisation. The meandering melody of a jazz number allowed him to indulge both his orderly, scientific side and also his freewheeling creativity. Ron could easily have built a career as a professional musician. As you'll see later, he combined his love for music with his work as an astronaut when he carried his saxophone into orbit and established yet another first in a life filled with breakthroughs.

Ron also began training in karate during his first year at A & T. Actually, we both entered the class, but I quickly decided that this was not my idea of fun. My brother's high threshold for pain, as well as his love for competition, made him a natural in the martial arts. Karate was the ideal sport for Ron. He never shied away from painful exercises, such as doing push ups on his knuckles. Blocking a blow with the forearm may look easy in those Kung-Fu movies, but in practice that maneuver leads to bruises and throbbing arms. At least, that was my experience, but that sort of thing didn't faze Ron. He simply shut out the pain and concentrated on the process.

I'm not the only one who felt that sparring brought more pain than satisfaction. That karate class began with an enrollment of two hundred students. As the weeks progressed, student after student dropped out of the grueling class. By the end of the semester, Ron was one of five remaining students. Before he graduated from A & T, he was good enough to become an instructor in his own right. Eventually Ron earned a sixth-degree black belt for his proficiency.

One day as Ron packed his gym bag for a workout, I said, "How do you find the time? I try to get to the gym, but I'm so busy."

Ron shrugged. "Karate is something I schedule, and everything else works around it," he said.

He wasn't prone to making excuses for himself. If something mattered to him, he made it a priority. He also found clever ways to squeeze the most out of every day. By teaching other students, my brother brought together his need for a regular workout and his love of teaching. As a karate instructor, he was demanding, insisting on the utmost effort from himself and his students. Those who studied under Ron appreciated his commitment and strove hard to meet his high expectations. He had a knack for getting more from people than they thought they could muster.

The passionate commitment to karate that began in our freshman year remained with him for the rest of his life. After his career moved him to a new city, he founded a new karate class and passed along his skill and know-how to others. I couldn't estimate how many people today are stronger and more confident thanks to Ron's karate classes and his devoted efforts to bring forth the best from every student.

Ron's enthusiasm for space exploration also continued unabated during our college years. Two especially critical aerospace events stood out during our days at A & T. On July 20, 1969, America finally seized the lead in the space race when *Apollo 11* successfully landed on the moon. Along with the rest of the civilized world, Ron and I were glued to the television, watching in awe as Neil Armstrong, clad in that bulky space suit, climbed down the ladder of the Lunar Excursion Module and became the first human being to set foot on the dusty lunar surface.

"That's one small step for man," Armstrong said, his voice scratchy and slightly distorted by transmission across the gulf of space, "and one giant leap for mankind."

This was like *Star Trek* come true, Buzz Aldrin and Neil Armstrong boldly going where no one had gone before.

The other event that captured global attention was equally heroic, if far less successful. Nine months after the amazing flight of Armstrong, Aldrin, and Collins, NASA launched *Apollo 13* on a follow-up mission. Unfortunately, en route *Apollo 13* suffered an explosion in the Command Module oxygen tank, and shortly afterward came the terse but frightening transmission: "Houston, we have a problem." The proposed lunar landing was aborted and ground control mounted a desperate, long-distance effort to rescue astronauts James Lovell, John Swigert, and Fred Haise.

A breathless world kept vigil for several harrowing days while the fate of the space voyagers remained uncertain. A commemorative medal later released by NASA pictures praying hands with the words *"Apollo 13...And The Whole World Prayed."* That statement is almost literally true. As thousands of Roman Catholics assembled at St. Peter's Basilica, Pope Paul prayed for the safe return of the astronauts. Jews gathered at the Wailing Wall in Jerusalem to intercede for the lives of the crewmen. At Chicago's Board of Trade, all sales halted while businessmen and speculators lifted up prayers on behalf of the space travelers. The day after the explosion the United States Senate approved a resolution urging all businesses and media broadcasters to pause at 9:00 P.M. so that people across the nation could join in prayer for the safety of the astronauts.

The damaged *Apollo 13* spacecraft limped back to earth and the crew survived in spite of staggering odds against their safe return. I cannot begin to understand why God says "yes" to some prayers and "no" to others, but the safe return of the *Apollo 13* proved to me that we are never beyond God's reach; even in the uttermost abyss of space He is still with us, both in life and in death.

Of course, not all the newsworthy events during our tenure at North Carolina A & T were so edifying. Those years represented a restless time in this country. The Vietnam War generated increasingly bitter protests as that seemingly interminable war dragged on with no victory in sight. Civil rights issues and the Vietnam War prompted marches, rallies, and acts of civil disobedience. The leaven of change that permeated the 1960s and 1970s particularly fomented unrest on college campuses, including Harvard, Stanford, Berkeley, and numerous historically black colleges and universities (HBCUs).

Student riots and protests were frequent occurrences during our college years at A & T. For instance, after the assassination of Dr. Martin Luther King, Jr., riots erupted on our campus so severe that school officials canceled classes and temporarily shut down the university to restore order. The memory of one particular riot is branded forever on my mind. On that occasion Ron and I came face to face with death. The events that followed forcefully reminded us of our mortality. The cause of the riot was something that makes no sense in retrospect; at nearby Dudley High School, a student had been disallowed the privilege of running for student body president, and angry ripples spread across our campus. I don't recall why the young man was removed from the ballot nor why this should have agitated students at A & T. Sometimes in those troubled days the most insignificant spark could ignite a powder keg of rebellion and violence.

At first those protests were sporadic and scattered. Not sensing the trouble in the air, I ambled over to the Student Union that evening to hang out with some friends. To my surprise, I found looters in the building, vandalizing and stealing school property as a mob mentality came upon our campus. Hysteria ran rampant. I wanted no part of that destructive and senseless behavior, so I backed out of the Student Union and returned to my dormitory, Scott Hall.

I bumped into my brother, and it was one of those rare moments when I turned out to be much smarter than him. I tried to talk him out of his reckless decision, but Ron thought maybe he could do some good among the looters. I told him what I'd seen but he decided to take a look for himself. Ron and a couple of his fellow karate friends, Ken and Sam, headed toward the Student Union. He hoped to calm the situation and convince the students to leave the building. He assumed he could count on his karate skills to defend himself if he had to scuffle, so my overly confident brother and his friends strode into the lion's den to be peacemakers.

Ron's decision almost resulted in tragedy. No sooner had Ron, Ken, and Sam entered the Student Union, the police arrived and burst into the building with weapons drawn.

"Raise your hands," an officer barked through a megaphone. "Up against the wall... right now!"

Ron and his friends complied with the command, pressing noses and palms against the block wall.

"What are we going to do?" Sam whispered fearfully.

"We'll explain everything to the cops," Ken said. "We didn't do anything wrong. They'll turn us loose."

"Sure they will," Sam said sarcastically. "They'll arrest everybody else, but when we tell them we're the good guys the police will let us go, yeah, right!"

"Man, we're gonna get kicked out of school," Ken moaned.

"Keep quiet," ordered the amplified voice of the police officer. "We'll get to you one at a time. Keep calm and we'll sort this out. You'll just make it worse for yourself if you resist arrest."

Ron stood at one end of the line of students, the exit door on his left and his friends on his right. My brother was not accustomed to being in trouble. He followed the rules and tried to do the right thing. That's why he was in this mess. After all, he wasn't there to tear up the building and loot the bookstore. He had come into the Student Union in hopes of pacifying the crowd, yet now he was about to go to jail.

Ron couldn't bear the thought of the police carting him off to the station, finger-printing him, and throwing him into a cell, especially when he had done nothing wrong. Something in his head told him to run. As I sit here in safety years later, I think Ron made a crazy choice when he decided to flee from the police. But I wasn't there at the time, and I can't fully appreciate how he felt or understand what thoughts raced through his mind. Foolish or not, my brother decided to make a break for freedom.

As inconspicuously as possible, he pulled his face from the wall and glanced in both directions. None of the authorities appeared to be looking in his direction. The door was only a few paces away. If he made a sudden break, he could be outside before anyone noticed—as long as no police were posted outside the door.

Spinning from the wall, Ron threw himself toward the exit. Instantly an angry voice rang out.

"Stop or I'll shoot!"

Ron continued to run and didn't look back. He just kept stride.

"Last warning!" the cop shouted. "Stop where you are!"

Again the inner voice, the voice of fear, clamored through Ron's mind.

"If he wants to stop me," Ron thought to himself, "he's going to have to shoot, because I'm not stopping."

Shoulders hunched against the expected impact of the bullet, he slammed against the panic bar and burst through the door into the night.

No officers kept watch on the walk outside, so he kept running. As he waited for the retort of a gun, his hearing became unnaturally acute. Ron heard the door smash against the wall, thrown so hard by his escape that it rebounded shut with a bang. Muffled shouts through the megaphone ordered students to get down on the floor. His own breathing and heartbeat roared in his ears. His pounding footfalls seemed as loud as drumbeats. But no gunfire exploded in the evening air.

My brother came within a hairsbreath of dying that evening. I'll never know what emotions surged through the police officer to keep him from squeezing the trigger. Perhaps he didn't have a clear shot. Maybe he realized that campus rowdiness wasn't adequate grounds for firing on a fleeing student. In moments of stress, people do not always make the wisest decision. When adrenaline is pumping, sometimes even the best-trained individuals take actions they later regret. My brother's foolish flight proves that to me. I am grateful that the police officer remained levelheaded. To this day, I thank God that my brother's life wasn't senselessly snuffed out that night because of one poor choice.

After Ron escaped the building, he sprinted across the parking lot. My room was the closest refuge he could count on, so he ran toward Scott Hall where we lived. Near the dormitory he crashed at full speed into a metal guy wire supporting a utility pole. Again, Providence watched over Ron. The heavy-gauge wire struck him squarely across the chest. Had he hit the wire a couple inches higher he would've caught the full force in his throat, crushing his windpipe.

I'd been outside watching for Ron and I saw him hit the wire. His legs flew into the air before him as the wire knocked him off his feet. He was so battered and exhausted that I had to pick him up from the ground and help him stagger into our dorm. How close Ron came to dying became clear to us as events unfolded through the rest of the night.

Shortly after Ron found a safe haven in my room, the National Guard arrived at our university. Personnel carriers rolled onto the campus grounds, unloading armed soldiers sent to restore order. I could hear gunfire and shouting in the darkness, but not until the next morning did I learn the full extent of the violence at our school.

When Ron and I entered Murphy Hall the next morning for breakfast, the dining hall fell utterly still and every eye fixed on me. Sentences trailed off, unfinished. Forks froze in mid-air. My friends stared at me as if I were a ghost newly risen from the grave. I didn't find out the cause of their consternation for several minutes, as everyone began talking at once.

When I pieced the story together, I found that, according to rumor, I had been shot and killed the night before. Even though I was unharmed, someone really had died from gunfire. The victim turned out to be a friend of mine, Willie Grimes. I was very saddened by this news. You see, Willie and I were both from the Carolinas, our builds and height were similar, and we both had pledged fraternities solo. In the confusion of the night before, friends mistakenly assumed that I was the one who'd been killed. Had the timing or circumstances been only slightly different, my brother or I might have been the one lying in a morgue the morning after the riots.

Ron's friends, Sam and Ken, were arrested that night and booked into jail the following morning. As a result of the charges against them they were both expelled from the university. My brother had narrowly escaped the same fate. With an expulsion from school, I'm certain Ron would never have made it into MIT, and I know that he would not have passed the intensive background check required of all potential astronauts. In short, my brother's poor decision on one tumultuous night might well have derailed all his plans, not to mention end his life outright.

It took Sam and Ken a year to clear their names of the charges. They, too, got another chance to return to college and graduated from universities in the Washington, D. C. area with degrees in computer science. Today, they have very successful careers as computer consultants and are married with beautiful families.

A single decision at a crucial moment can change the entire direction of a lifetime for good or for bad. My heart is unshakably convinced that Ron and his future achievements survived that night because God watched over him. Sometimes He overrules our failings and maintains His own plans for us regardless of our mistakes. This was another reminder that we don't have the final word on the outcome of our decisions.

I don't want to build up my brother into someone bigger than he was in real life. I'm telling this story so others can see that Ron was as human and fallible as the rest of us. My brother had a deep faith in God, and God knew that what was in Ron's heart that night was his desire to make peace in a dangerous situation. God's hand was on my brother to preserve him and bring him safely through that crisis in spite of his poor choice. God had a purpose for Ron, so He stepped in to give help when it was most needed.

If we were held accountable for every mistake, every failure of judgment, every lapse in good sense, few of us could justify ourselves. God's mercy offers us second chances, and divine forgiveness sometimes allows us to walk away from honest mistakes unscathed. He doesn't want to see any life squandered, not Ron's, not yours, not mine. After all, God has a purpose for you, too.

CHAPTER 9

Quitting Is Not An Option

Ron and I graduated from North Carolina A & T in the spring of 1971. He earned a degree in physics and graduated magna cum laude. I earned a degree in Industrial Technology minus the fancy Latin words. At first I considered going to work for Kaiser Aluminum in Louisiana, but then Polaroid Corporation offered me a position in the Boston area. Heading north didn't appeal to me, but as I deliberated, Ron made me an offer I couldn't refuse.

"Why don't you come to Boston?" he asked. "We can be roommates and get an apartment not too far from either your job or MIT where I'll be working on my doctorate."

"I don't know," I told him. "Those Boston winters have to be tough on Southerners."

"Nah. It's not that bad," Ron insisted. "I know of a really nice apartment on Columbus Avenue near the center of downtown Boston. It's about a mile from the Charles River. The church owns the apartment building so the rent is cheap. Here is the best part— you still get to see my face everyday."

"You were doing okay until you mentioned your face," I laughed. "Okay, I'll take the job with Polaroid, but you'd better have a good heating system in that apartment." Quite frankly, I was ecstatic that Ron and I would be a team again and I knew he was, too. We had been together so long I couldn't imagine him not being around.

Graduating from the Massachusetts Institute of Technology is a extremely impressive accomplishment, but even being admitted is no small feat. MIT accepted Ron into its graduate program for several reasons. His academic showing at A & T proved that he was capable of top-notch scholarship. Also, he had already established relationships with professors and faculty at MIT by virtue of his participation in the exchange program. In a sense, he already had one foot in the door. Knowing Ron personally convinced decision-makers at MIT that he was dedicated to excellence and hard work.

Dr. Sandin at A & T was instrumental in obtaining the Ford Foundation Fellowship that made Ron's tenure at MIT possible.

"If you can't give the Ford fellowship to Ron McNair you can't give it to anyone," Dr. Sandin wrote in a letter of recommendation.

Ron also benefited from the general move toward affirmative action that gained momentum in the early 1970s. But no one gave him a free ride to a Ph.D. He was certainly qualified to do the work. Once he got into MIT he had to meet the standards of the school or he wouldn't last very long. Nevertheless, Ron's story exemplifies the wisdom of opening the door for minorities at top schools. Many students from economically disadvantaged backgrounds do not realize their full potential because of their lack of accessibility to higher education. Affirmative Action isn't about preferential treatment; it's about fairness. America can't afford to kick-to-the-curb any of its intellectual capital. Ron McNair proved that.

In spite of MIT's good intention of providing access to promising students like my brother, some students were antagonistic because they felt that Ron had taken a slot that should have gone to a better-qualified white student. Overall, he felt welcomed at MIT and made many close friends there, among both students and faculty. Nevertheless, we both experienced a kind of racism in Boston, unlike anything that we'd faced in the South. Admittedly, the society in Lake City expected us to know our place and stay there; even so, we seldom heard racial slurs spoken behind our backs as was often the case when we strolled through white neighborhoods in and around Boston during the '70s. I believe that the new bussing laws that were being instituted at the time in Boston and vicinity brought the worse out of everyone, black and white. Bussing meant, for the most part, that some black students would be bussed to predominantly white schools to encourage educational and racial equality in public schools. But bussing stirred up a racial hornet's nest.

Once, while practicing his karate in a public park, Ron had to flee from a gang of white youths. On another occasion, my car was stolen and vandalized, with hateful racist epithets etched in the hood. We'd believed we were moving to the cradle of liberty in Boston, and we were disillusioned to find how misplaced our expectations were.

We tried not to take such things to heart. For Ron, racial prejudice provided one more reason to knuckle down and do his best work. He had no intention of letting others define his possibilities or determine his limits. If being black meant he had to work harder to succeed, that's what he would do without complaint. In fact, that lesson had been instilled in both of us from our earliest days. Both our parents and our teachers drummed into our heads the realization that we had to work even harder than white students if we were going to prove ourselves.

The attitudes of a few ignorant people did nothing to dim Ron's overall excitement at formally matriculating at MIT. Without question, he was studying at one of the finest and most prestigious schools in the world. No student could approach the sweeping steps of the pillared administration building at MIT without at least a twinge of intimidation. Never before had Ron worked in the company of such brilliant students. For instance, two graduate students of our acquaintance had invented sophisticated telephone tampering devices in their spare time. They tinkered together a wire contrivance called a Spiro that allowed them to make long distance calls at no cost. A second invention, a black box dubbed the Agnew, allowed a telephone to receive long-distance calls without the caller being billed. The Agnew fooled the phone company into thinking that the receiving telephone had never been answered. Notwithstanding the ethics of those innovations, their technical aspects indicate the caliber of student drawn to MIT.

I spent a lot of my free time on MIT's campus with my brother and his friends, and I gained a clear impression of the university. For the geniuses of MIT, the workload was staggering, and even in the wee hours labs were lighted for night owls struggling to keep up with the merciless pace of their courses. I didn't envy Ron, but he leaped eagerly into the challenges of obtaining a Ph.D., spending long hours in the lab that we called "the dungeon." His area of special concentration was optical physics, specifically lasers. In his years at MIT, he did research with Dr. Ali Javan, who was the inventor of the gas laser, and also with his advisor, Dr. Michael Feld.

Ron sometimes lifted his nose from the grindstone. I never understood how he could juggle so many balls at once, but even with his heavy academic load, my brother enjoyed himself and maintained a social life. As he had done at A & T, he gathered like-minded friends around himself. He had a circle of physics colleagues, buddies from the Black Student Union, and friends at St. Paul AME Church, just down the street from MIT.

Connecting with a local church congregation was one of Ron's first priorities upon arriving in Cambridge. No matter where he found himself, throughout his life he always sought out the church. He wasn't one of those people who just pay lip service to their beliefs, showing up on Sunday morning and ignoring the church the next six days. His Christian faith was a crucial and fundamental aspect of his life. He didn't talk about his faith constantly the way some people do, but he always tried to put his spiritual beliefs into action. Once we were at a friend's party and stayed until 4:00 A.M. on Sunday morning.

Ron came into my bedroom around 8:00 A.M. "You're going to church, man?", Ron asked.

With sleep still in my eyes, I mumbled, "Ah, I guess so." I was hoping he would say 'let's pass this Sunday.'

He believed in serving in the church. He hadn't been

attending St. Paul AME very long when he started the Karate Club in the fellowship hall. Ron was a very good karate instructor who worked with students at all levels. Experienced karate devotees were welcome; so were elementary school kids with no experience. Before long the parents of those kids were also jumping into the fun. For instance, Dr. Michael Feld, his advisor, brought his twin sons, Jonathan and David, to try out the class and soon Dr. Feld joined as well. Ron's karate classes were a rich mix of ages, races, and even faiths. The members of St. Paul began calling him the Minister of Defense, a title that both amused and delighted him.

As is often the case, his commitment to serving others at St. Paul led to a rich blessing for Ron himself. One night at a church-sponsored potluck dinner for singles, he met his wife-to-be. Cheryl Moore was a beautiful young teacher from Jamaica, New York. She and Ron hit it off from their first conversation. I could tell that my brother was seriously smitten and I wasn't surprised that only a brief courtship preceded their wedding.

Cheryl and Ron married during his last year at MIT. He made me his best man at their wedding, a role I took very seriously.

"Carl, you'll be my best man, chauffeur, and general factotum." Which was a glorified way of saying I was his gofer.

The wedding still lives in my memory, one of those shining moments undimmed by the passage of years. Naturally, Ron would be my best man at my wedding a few years later. I returned the favor and gave him the honor of being my "general factotum."

The joy of Ron and Cheryl's wedding stands in stark contrast to another event that took place during his final year at MIT. By that point in his academic career, he had compiled a massive amount of research data in preparation for writing his doctoral dissertation. The late nights and endless hours of experimentation in the laboratory had generated enough notebooks and computer keypunch cards to stuff a large suitcase. For convenience, Ron actually carried his data and notes in an Army duffle bag that rarely left his sight.

Ron's lab was just across the street from the Charles River. One sunny day, he and Cheryl decided to go for a stroll along the riverside. Inexplicably, Ron set down his precious duffle bag—the one containing all his experimental results—on the sidewalk while they made their way down to the riverbank. Afterwards, Ron insisted he'd only left the bag for a few minutes, but when he returned from the waterside it was gone. Someone had picked up the bag and walked away with it.

"Oh no! This is terrible," Cheryl lamented, nearly hysterical at the loss. "Maybe someone thought the bag was lost. They might turn it in."

"Maybe," Ron said, looking up and down the sidewalk. "But I wouldn't count on it."

"What if it's really gone?" Cheryl asked. "So much work. All those years."

Ron remained outwardly calm. Staring into the distance, he said, "Let me think for a while."

He never saw the duffle bag again. After finding nothing of monetary value, the thief probably emptied Ron's hard earned data into the trash. Regardless of his outward demeanor, I know my brother was crushed by this circumstance. Many people would never have recovered from such a catastrophe. I was both shocked and heartbroken by Ron's disastrous loss. This could add another year or more to his graduation date in the doctoral program.

"What will you do now?" I asked him.

His answer was simple and straightforward, a distillation of his philosophy of life.

"I'm not sure," he admitted, "but quitting is not an option."

Those few words capture my brother's personality.

Quitting is not an option.

Ron was a brilliant and richly gifted man, but many gifted people never achieve much in life. They coast on their talents, they pursue the path of least resistance, and they never apply their genius with honest sweat. Natural talents notwithstanding, such people never rise very high. More than any other single factor, this philosophy was the quality that set my brother apart. His work ethic, his competitive spirit, his passion for challenges all sprang from a deep commitment to persevere. When others surrendered, Ron kept pushing. When those around him threw in the towel, he simply worked harder, stayed up later, and accomplished more. When quitting is not an alternative, the only option that remains is success.

Ron went back to the lab and began repeating his experiments. He labored systematically and carefully. The energy that might have been squandered in self-pity or rage, Ron funneled into his research. When the duffle bag disappeared, Ron lost at least three years of data, information painstakingly garnered from hundreds of experiments. Incredibly, he replicated the three years of data in a mere three months of intensive effort.

The lost duffle bag was not the only occasion when I saw Ron's indomitable spirit battle through a crisis. Somewhat earlier during his studies, my brother faced the dreaded General Exam, a grueling rite of passage required of all Ph.D. candidates at MIT. The General Exam was a comprehensive test with five parts. The test covered all the information a student was expected to master in his particular program, even including the student's undergraduate studies prior to arriving at MIT.

The General Exam was an essential step toward a Doctor of Philosophy degree. According to my brother's former study partner at MIT, Dr. Sylvester (Jim) Gates, the "Generals, or qualifying examination" was the "gatekeeper" that stood mercilessly between them and the coveted Ph.D. Jim admits that he took part one of the five-part exam and failed miserably the first time. Today, Jim is an internationally renowned physicist at the University of Maryland, College Park.

No candidate could sidestep this brain-curdling, spirit-crushing series of tests. Ron prepared for the General Exam in his usual thorough fashion. Nevertheless, he failed the test on his first try, too. Disappointed but undaunted, my brother waited the obligatory six months between tests, studied even harder, and took the General Exam a second time.

He flunked once again.

A few doctoral candidates succumbed to panic after their second failure, but not Ron. He registered for the next exam and went back to the books. Naturally, the normal course work continues while students ready themselves for the General Exam. He couldn't simply drop everything else and cram for the make-or-break test, so he added General Exam preparation on top of his already grueling schedule.

Although Ron was normally stoic about setbacks, his bitter disappointment was apparent to me when he failed the General Exam for the third time. Even so, he never considered cutting his losses and settling for a master's degree or transferring to a less demanding university. As usual, quitting was not an option for Ronald McNair.

Ron went to the chair of his department to find out exactly what mistakes he'd made on the exam. He reasoned that if he knew where his performance was weak, he could concentrate on those areas. The physics chairperson promised to personally review Ron's exams. What happened next seemed odd to me at the time, and even now I don't entirely understand the chain of events. A few weeks after that meeting, my brother learned that that he had in fact passed his third attempt at the General Exam. The physics chair explained to my brother that, having reviewed the scoring on the test, he could find no plausible reason for failing him. Consequently, the chairperson awarded Ron a passing score.

I was impressed once again by my brother's refusal to accept defeat. What if he had quit after the second failure? What if he'd been so dispirited by his third exam results that he'd never approached the department chair? Consider the tragic irony if Ron had passed the third General Exam and never found out because he gave up in discouragement and abandoned his hopes of earning a Ph.D. What a terrible waste that would have been! Looking back, I can only be grateful for his stubborn philosophy: *Quitting is not an option.*

In 1976, Ron graduated from the Massachusetts Institute of Technology with a Ph.D. in laser physics. Nine years and eleven months earlier, in a Carver High School essay titled "Ten Years Hence," he'd committed himself to a ten-year deadline for becoming Dr. Ronald E. McNair. Miraculously, at the age of twenty-six he reached his goal, achieving it with one month to spare.

CHAPTER 10

—

The Astronaut Candidate

After graduation from MIT, Ron and Cheryl moved to California, where he took a job with Hughes Research Laboratories in Malibu. He was in California for two years while I remained in Boston. We kept in touch, of course, but we had most of America between us, so we didn't see as much of each other as we'd have liked. As was his custom, he found a church in Los Angeles, Trinity Baptist Church, and soon became actively involved there. He once again set himself up as the Minister of Defense at the church and started a new karate class that became as popular as the one back in Cambridge.

Ron and Cheryl enjoyed the California life. Their years there were a welcome time of respite and renewal. For someone as active and athletic as Ron, the West Coast weather and varied terrain were great joys, especially after spending so many years buried like a mole in "the dungeon" at MIT.

He immersed himself in his field of expertise, working at Hughes on optical and laser projects. He was certainly happy in his marriage. After the punishing pace of MIT, the couple actually had more time to enjoy one another. From all outward appearances, the good life had arrived, an overdue gravy train earned and fully paid for by many years of hard work and selfless determination. This should have been a time of contented bliss. He finally had everything he'd striven for. Ron's success was living proof that dreams come true.

Nevertheless, I sensed a restlessness in him. Perhaps working so strenuously for so many years at MIT only wetted his insatiable appetite for scientific discovery. For a decade Ron had struggled toward a clearly and defined goal—a doctorate in physics. Having achieved that calling, I wondered if he needed a new, equally challenging objective.

His work at Hughes was exciting, but maybe the shift into a five-day work week routine felt like a step toward the humdrum. Sometimes the period following a great accomplishment is anticlimactic. Life was good, but where was the adrenaline rush? Where was the all-consuming competition?

Not that Ron ever confessed such feelings to me; he didn't have to. I knew how he was put together. After watching him surmount one obstacle after another since childhood, I understood that he couldn't be content on the plateau. Most people would be happy to savor the mountaintop after the long climb, but not Ron. No sooner did he reach an arduous peak than he was searching the horizon for a loftier mountain to scale. I fully expected him to find a new challenge soon, but even I was surprised by what he chose next.

He called me one afternoon in 1977. We chitchatted for a few minutes about work and family; then, after a momentary pause, he said, "I don't know if I should tell you this, but I'm going to be an astronaut."

I didn't think my brother had any surprises left, at least not for me. With anyone else I would have taken the statement for a joke, but Ron wasn't just anyone.

"You're going to be a what?" I asked.

Given my surprise, that was the cleverest response I could muster.

"An astronaut," he said. "I'm going to work for NASA."

"When did this happen?" I asked him.

"It hasn't actually happened yet," Ron admitted. "I got a brochure in the mail explaining that NASA was looking to recruit a new corps of astronauts for the new Space Shuttle program."

"Yeah, I heard about that program. So?"

"I know they're hoping to bring in more women and minorities. So I applied."

"But how do you know you'll be selected?" I asked, thinking of larger-than-life heroes like Neil Armstrong and John Glenn.

"I told you I applied."

"You've worn glasses as long as I can remember," I reminded him. "Astronauts have to have 20/20 vision, don't they?"

I visualized his shrug on the other end of the phone line.

"I'm not applying to become a pilot," he said. "I'd be a mission specialist, doing scientific experiments and gathering technical data. My vision won't be a problem."

"You sound like you're already being fitted for a space suit," I kidded him. "What makes you think you'll get in?"

"I told you, I sent in the application forms," he explained patiently. "I've already applied."

"And that's that?" I asked. "You filled out some papers, and now you're going to be an astronaut?"

Even after so many years of living with Ron, his matter-of-fact confidence staggered me.

"How many other people do you figure have applied?" I wondered aloud.

"The mailing I received was sent to over 9,000 people," Ron said nonchalantly. "I'm sure others have heard about the search from television and radio. It's a dream job, and NASA hasn't brought in any new astronauts for almost ten years. I'd guess something like 10,000 people might be applying."

I found out later that his estimate was too low. The real number was slightly over 11,000, from which NASA would select only thirty-five astronaut candidates. He remained utterly indifferent to those near- impossible odds. Was he even listening to his own words? I made one more stab at talking some sense of reality into his hard head.

"With so many people beating on their door," I said, "why should NASA make you an astronaut?"

"Why not?" he asked. I heard mild surprise in his voice. "I have the credentials."

I started to laugh.

"Either you're absolutely, certifiably crazy," I said, "or you have more faith than anyone I've ever met."

He laughed, too.

"I'll let you know when I hear from NASA," he promised.

"Just send me a postcard from the moon," I said.

The whole thing sounded to me like an impossible dream. I decided that my brother had finally overreached himself. We were just ordinary guys from Lake City, South Carolina. Black people didn't go rocketing into outer space. We logged in our forty hours a week, barbecued on Sunday afternoons, and hoped to pay off the mortgage before we retired. Maybe we would make a trip to Disney World every now and then, but that's the only other world we would visit.

I was concerned about Ron. He clearly had high hopes for a career as an astronaut. He wasn't used to failure, and I wasn't sure how he'd handle the disappointment. I made a mental note to keep in closer touch with him for the next few months.

When we saw each other at Christmas I asked a few open-ended questions and confirmed that he still clung to his dream of going into space as a mission specialist. I made bland comments about how many applicants there were and how few positions were available. I was planting seeds so that Ron would know I was available to talk about this anytime he wanted. I wanted to be there for my brother when reality came crashing in on his head.

Not long after Christmas, in early January 1978, I turned on the television in the middle of the day. I was just in time to catch a special news bulletin. Walter Cronkite announced that the National Aeronautics and Space Administration had recruited "the most recent corps of astronauts to carry on America's brave tradition of space exploration." From roughly

11,000 applicants, NASA had selected thirty-five individuals to enter the training program.

Poor Ron. This was going to be such a bitter blow.

"Congratulations and Godspeed to the newest generation of astronauts," Cronkite said with an affable smile. Then he read the list of names.

"Guion S. Bluford, Jr., Daniel C. Brandenstein, James F. Buchli, Michael L. Coats, Richard O. Covey…"

Ron must not have made the cut. He would've called to alert me. Even so, I couldn't help but listen to the litany of names.

"…Robert L. Gibson, John M. Fabian, Anna L. Fisher, Dale A. Gardner…"

True to its public intent, NASA had obviously broadened the guidelines for astronaut selection. I heard the names of several women on the list. I wondered how many minority members might be in this class.

"…Terry J. Hart, Frederick H. Hauck…"

Thirty-five winners out of 11,000 applicants. I leaned closer to the television screen, drawn like the moths that used to flutter around our porch light on summer nights back in Lake City.

"…Steven A. Hawley, Jeffrey A. Hoffman, Shannon W. Lucid…"

Obviously the list of astronauts was alphabetical. As the announcer moved closer to the middle of the alphabet my heart was pounding so hard I had to turn up the volume. Why was I so excited? Ron's name couldn't be on NASA's list.

"...Jon A. McBride..."

"No way. Not a chance in the world," I whispered.

"Ronald E. McNair," Walter Cronkite said.

I sat before the television screen with wide eyes and gaping mouth. I didn't hear another word from the announcer's mouth, not a single name that followed Ron's. Somehow I felt two utterly opposite emotions simultaneously.

"Oh my God, oh my God, oh my God", I shouted in a daze.

I was in shock at this too-good-to-be-true news. My brother, the guy I had shared a bed with for all those years in that leaky house on Moore Street, was going to be an astronaut. He had beaten the impossible odds. The guy who cropped tobacco at my side was going to outer space!

At the same time, I felt no surprise at all, as if this was the natural and inevitable outcome of Ron's aspirations. In spite of my outward protests, perhaps some corner of my mind had known all along that if my brother truly wanted to be an astronaut, he would be.

I ran for the telephone to call Ron. My hand was trembling and I had to try twice before I dialed the number correctly. When I heard the familiar voice on the line, I shouted, "Congratulations!"

"What are you talking about?"

"You're in," I said. My voice was still too loud, but I didn't care.

"What do you mean I'm in?

"You made the astronaut program!"

"I did?" There was a slight pause while he pondered this information. "Let me see what I can find out. I'll call you back," he said.

Incredibly, I'd heard the news first. Somehow my brother's name was released to the press before he was formally notified. My phone call apparently caught him off guard.

The announcement that he'd made the final list didn't come entirely out of the blue. Ron was aware that NASA had conducted a rigorous security check of his background. Friends had phoned to say that Space Agency officials had been asking questions about his personality and relationships. That he remained under consideration to that point was encouraging. The majority of the would-be astronauts were eliminated long before the time-consuming background scrutiny.

Even more telling, the Agency had flown Ron to Texas for a personal interview. For several months, NASA summoned groups of twenty finalists for conversations, ten such groups altogether. Most of the hopefuls never got as far as the face-to-face interview. Ron was asked to write an essay about why he wanted to be an astronaut, and his written answer was read beforehand by an interview committee. He told me the interview was casual, an informal meeting with fifteen to twenty people in a conference room. Their questions ranged from every direction - professional, personal, technical, theoretical, serious, and humorous. Ron also underwent a thorough physical exam on that trip and met with two psychiatrists for psychological evaluation.

"If those psychiatrists were on the ball, they'd have pitched you out the door after the first question," I kidded him. "They should've called me. I could tell them some things."

"I know a few things about you, too," Ron assured me. "I'll keep quiet if you will."

"What did they ask you?"

"We talked about all kinds of stuff," Ron said. "I got the impression they're looking for team players. They tried to figure out if I could get along with other people."

"Sure," I said. "That makes sense. If you're going to be cooped up together in a spaceship, you need crewmembers who won't drive each other crazy."

"Especially under stressful conditions," Ron added. "With delicate maneuvers and intricate experiments under way, NASA doesn't want clashing personalities derailing the mission."

Recalling how far Ron had come in the review process, I knew the news I gave him on the phone couldn't have come as a complete shock. He'd had indications that he was on the short list of candidates. Was he merely astonished that I'd gotten word before he did? Or was he genuinely amazed to be chosen? I smiled at the surprise I heard in his voice. Maybe his self-confidence wasn't as unshakable as it appeared.

My family nearly exploded with pride. Dad spread the word to everyone he knew, and probably bragged to a few strangers, too. He invited his friends to a party at a restaurant near his home in order to celebrate "my son the astronaut." Mom was proud and excited as well, but also nervous and a little worried. Her baby was going to be strapped into a rocket and fired into space.

This was the biggest excitement to ever hit the McNair

family. For that matter, nothing this monumental had ever emerged from Lake City. The whole town was buzzing with the news. People on the street asked one another, "Have you heard about that McNair boy?"

Long-time friends swapped stories about their shenanigans with my brother from the "old days."

"We should have seen this coming," they said.

"Remember how he talked about Sputnik until he nearly drove us crazy?"

"He was always into science fiction. He used to read those space-monster comic books at the drugstore. And he'd knock you down to get home in time for *Star Trek*."

Back at Carver High, teachers assured one another that they'd always known Ron was going places.

Mrs. Connors said, "I never saw Ron in any seat except the front desk. When he missed a test question he couldn't rest until he found out what was wrong with his answer."

"I'm planning a series of lessons on Ron. These children need to see what a person can do when they put their best foot forward," mused Mrs. Porter-Green.

I wouldn't have been surprised to learn that they were reminiscing at the public library about the day Ron checked out those science and calculus books.

"I was in the library that day. I saw the whole thing. He was a puny little thing, but you could tell there was something special about him. I could see it in his eyes."

Ron's success story belonged to the whole town. Even Lake

City citizens who'd never met him in their lives laid claim to this hometown hero. He was one of us. He'd walked our streets, gone to our movie theater, sweated in the fields like everybody else. Folks could point to the pew he used to sit in every Sunday. That auto body shop around the corner, that's where his dad used to work. Even though Ron had left town, you might go out for a loaf of bread and bump into his mother or one of his aunts.

When Ron went into space, he knew he wouldn't be going alone. The whole town would hitch a ride with this hometown hero, at least in spirit. We felt that this trip to the stars belonged to all of us. This was a success story, an American Dream, for hard-working people, ordinary people. No matter how far a person travels in life or how high one climbs on the ladder of achievement, no one truly leaves the old hometown behind. Our childhood home is the place we always carry with us. Ron came from Lake City, and when he rocketed into outer space he would take Lake City with him.

CHAPTER 11

—

Earning His Wings

Ron reported to Johnson Space Center in Houston, Texas for his initial orientation in February 1978. The meeting provided him with his first opportunity to meet the other members of his class, as well as twenty-eight other astronaut candidates who were already in training. During that meeting, technicians measured the so-called AsCans—astronaut candidates—for their flight suits and T-38 flight helmets. Actually being fitted for a space suit made the whole adventure suddenly become real for Ron. This was no fantasy. He was actually preparing for space travel.

Many long hours of physical and mental training lay ahead before Ron would earn the silver pin that signified his completion of training. Then he'd continue to wait and prepare for the mission that would earn him a gold pin, the sign of an astronaut who'd actually been in space. Nevertheless, regardless of the hurdles ahead, my brother was on his way to the stars.

Ron and Cheryl left Malibu, California and moved to Houston, where he began his training in July. At that time, their family still consisted of only the two of them. They started out in an apartment until they could get their feet on the ground. Later they bought a home in Clear Lake, a community just outside of Houston. From the windows of that house they could see the nearby space center. After two or three years in Clear Lake, they moved to another home a few miles away, in what Ron called a "space neighborhood," where most of their neighbors worked in some branch of the aerospace industry.

Ron and Cheryl had two children after moving to Houston. Their firstborn was a healthy baby boy who they named Reginald. Two years later Cheryl gave birth to their daughter, Joy. My niece's name was apt because Ron's children were an endless source of joy for him. He made time every day after work to play with his kids, and the children came to expect that romping time with their dad.

My brother loved to take his children with him whenever feasible, both so that he could enjoy time with them and show them off to his friends and colleagues. For instance, he took little Reggie to a karate class when he was only two months old. In a press conference one day, Ron stood before the cameras holding Reggie by the hand as he told reporters, "My son is already an astronaut. He's just waiting for his first flight assignment."

Ron belonged to an unusually large class of astronauts, the largest ever selected up to that time. Of the thirty-five astronauts in training, only fifteen were pilots. The remaining twenty were mission specialists, highly educated scientists and engineers, trained to carry out various specialized tasks on shuttle flights. Those numbers reflected NASA's trend of moving away from exclusively choosing "flight jockeys" to emphasize and include candidates with scientific educational credentials as well.

Aside from sheer size, the class of 1978 was unusual in other regards. Unlike earlier groups of recruits, these thirty-five individuals were selected specifically to fly shuttle flights. NASA was eager to make space flight profitable — or, at least financially sustainable. The shuttle program seemed the best way to accomplish that goal. The shuttles were capable of placing satellites in orbit for corporations and foreign governments—for a fee. Should those satellites malfunction at some future date, shuttle crews could also recover them for repair, again at a cost. NASA hoped that this revenue would shift the cost of the space program from the taxpayer to eventually allow the private sector to defray the immense expense of space exploration.

Ron's class of astronauts was also the most diverse in history. No longer was space the exclusive domain of military guys. This group included a liberal mix of civilians—nearly half—as well as six women and four members who represented minorities. Several "firsts" came out of the Class of 1978. The first African-American in space was one of Ron's classmates, Guion Bluford. Sally Ride was the first American woman in space. Kathryn Sullivan became the first American woman to participate in an Extra-Vehicular Activity, and Shannon Lucid set the women's record for most continuous time in space.

In 1981, a fellow South Carolinian and our Omega Psi Phi fraternity brother, Charles Bolden, Jr. became the fourth African-American astronaut in the space shuttle program.

This group would dominate the shuttle program for years to come. Between 1983 and 1992 one or more members of that class flew with each shuttle mission. All thirty-five astronauts made at least one shuttle flight. The majority went into space more than once. From a later class, Dr. Mae Jemison became the first African-American female in space in 1992.

Although NASA doesn't insist on it, some of the astronaut classes have created nicknames for themselves. Mindful that they represented the first generation of astronauts trained specifically for shuttle flight, Ron's class started calling itself the "Thirty-Five New Guys" or the TFNG's for short.

Guy Bluford came up with the idea of getting a class "patch," and he approached Robert McCall to create a design for them. McCall, a famous space artist, painted a shuttle soaring majestically skyward, leaving the earth far below. On the left side of the shuttle the sun shone on the numeral "35". On the other side of the shuttle the date "1978" hung in a dark, starry sky.

The group even came up with its own t-shirt, designed by classmate Judy Resnik. The shirt showed an intricate drawing of the shuttle in space with thirty-five space-suited figures crowded on and around the vehicle, carrying out a multitude of scientific tasks. Underneath the drawing were the large letters "TFNG" and beneath that in smaller letters the unofficial team motto: "We Deliver."

Once Ron got started at the Space Center, I thought he'd tell me endless stories about the difficult astronaut training regimen, but he never complained. In fact, he played down the physical aspects of his preparation, assuring me that the program wasn't all that strenuous. At the time, I assumed he was understating the difficulties as he often did, but later I realized that a couple of factors probably did make his training relatively painless. For one thing, Ron was in excellent physical condition. He'd been a natural athlete since childhood, and he continued faithfully in his karate workouts.

Also, the physical conditioning required by NASA simply wasn't as demanding in 1978 as it had been in the earlier days of the space program. When the first astronauts were undergoing preparation, science didn't have a clear idea of what their bodies would be subjected to in achieving escape velocity and living in weightlessness. Those first astronauts over-trained in order to be on the safe side. Experience had clarified what astronauts could expect to encounter. Also improved launch technology had somewhat eased the physical stress of escaping earth's gravitation.

Of course, the training involved far more than physical conditioning. Ron told me that he spent seemingly endless hours in classroom instruction, covering courses in astronomy, aerodynamics, biology, physiology, orbital mechanics, and even geology. The AsCans poured over schematics of shuttle design and wiring diagrams. Much of the training was hands-on and participatory. Ron and the others practiced in a variety of simulators designed to give the "feel" of space travel without actually leaving the ground. Pilots specialized in flight simulators and mission specialists, like Ron, worked more with the Remote Manipulator System to learn how to operate the "mechanical arm" that would place satellites in orbit.

Ron spent considerable time in a huge tank of water where he learned spacesuit operation in an environment that approximated airless weightlessness. Before the AsCans could even begin spacesuit training in the tank, they received scuba instruction and were required to maintain scuba proficiency as part of their responsibility as mission specialists.

Ron and the others experienced genuine—if brief—
moments of weightlessness while training in the modified
KC-135 jet aircraft, known as the "vomit comet." During
zero-gravity simulations the jet cuts power and literally falls
thousands of feet toward the earth. During these periods of
free-fall, the passengers "float" inside the plane, experiencing
a kind of weightlessness. A trainer led Ron though free-fall
exercises to acclimate him to the kind of conditions that
awaited him in orbit.

NASA also sent the AsCans on frequent field trips. They
visited the Houston Planetarium several times, and received
geology training during a trip to the Arizona desert. The
TFNG's went to the Vance Air Force Base in Oklahoma for
survival school. The group visited most of NASA's installations,
including the headquarters in Washington, D.C. and the Jet
Propulsion Laboratory in Pasadena, California. During a trip
to Rockwell International Corporation, the AsCans saw the
unfinished space shuttles in the process of assembly. A trek to
Cape Canaveral, Florida, in December 1978 provided one of
the most thrilling moments in the long training program. At
the Cape, the AsCans witnessed first-hand an actual rocket
launch, imagining themselves aboard that thundering colossus,
riding a shaft of flame into the sky.

Although NASA originally estimated a training period
of roughly two years, Ron could tell that the agency had a
pressing need for more astronauts in the near future. In those
busy days there were more jobs for astronauts than program
graduates to fill those jobs. Perhaps because of that necessity,
Ron and his colleagues spent only one year in training, instead
of the originally projected two years. At the conclusion of their

studies, they received their silver pins, and NASA declared them ready for duty.

Typically for my brother, even with so much intensive activity going on at NASA, he found time for life outside his work. During his stay in Houston he taught physics for a while at Texas Southern University. Ron loved teaching and he was in his element in the classroom. He found that sharing knowledge with others was immensely fulfilling.

Of course, he and Cheryl found a church in Houston. He never neglected his faith, and always sought a church home wherever he settled. Predictably, he soon had a karate class up and kicking in the Wheeler Avenue Baptist Church.

He also indulged his passion for music. He spent time with his beloved saxophone and got into a band made up of amateur musicians from the space center. He didn't mention it to anyone yet, but he was already making plans for the first outer space saxophone concert. Since Ron had once refused to board an airplane without his saxophone, maybe he'd try the same stunt on the shuttle.

Unofficially, I've heard that Ron was probably in line to be the first African-American in space, but events conspired to change that scenario. In 1982, while Ron and Cheryl were driving across the Texas countryside on the interstate highway, a pickup truck rear-ended their car. The accident was especially frightening because Cheryl was pregnant at the time. Both my brother and my sister-in-law were knocked unconscious by the impact. Fortunately, Cheryl was otherwise unhurt and her unborn baby came through without any problems.

On the other hand, Ron bore the brunt of the injuries. As on several occasions in the past, he once again had to deal with painful damage. He had broken ribs as well as internal injuries.

More troubling, a head trauma left him with persistent double vision. Over time he recovered fully, but in the interim his slowly healing ribs and lingering vision problem removed him from the mission rotation. He was off the flight list for most of the following year when Guion "Guy" Bluford became the first African-American to reach outer space in 1983.

I don't know for certain that Ron would have been first, but he was certainly moving on an accelerated schedule. To be honest, I would have liked to see that honor go to him. There aren't that many firsts in life, and to be the first black astronaut in space would have been a remarkable honor, a moment in history inscribed with the name of Ronald McNair. Knowing Ron, I'm sure that mattered more to me than it did to him. In fact, Guy Bluford later mentioned that Ron had called to wish him well on the night before his historic first flight on the STS-8 mission. The phone call and his sincere good wishes truly touched Guy.

For my brother, achievement counted far more than recognition. If anything, he went out of his way to avoid interviews and publicity. Reporters often characterized him as the shy or soft-spoken astronaut. Ron was in the space program to challenge himself and offer his best work. He wanted to go where he'd never gone before and stretch both his horizons and personal limits. He loved learning new things, so the NASA training was an intellectual playground for him. Whether anyone took note of his accomplishments didn't matter, the achievements counted for just as much even if no one noticed. Setting records or winning accolades along the way simply didn't excite him. He knew the importance of what he was doing, and that was enough.

CHAPTER 12

————

Maiden Voyage

Everyone in the McNair family felt that our lives had been electrified when we got word that Ron would fly on board the *Challenger* on Space Shuttle Mission 41-B scheduled for launch in early 1984. To the uninitiated that may seem a long wait for his first flight, but he was actually moving quickly through the process. Selected in 1978 and training completed in 1979, Ron was on the NASA fast track. Many potential astronauts have waited far longer for their freshman mission in space.

Ron re-entered specialized training for the flight, and as the launch date drew nearer, his preparations became more intense and demanding. The final six months were particularly hectic and crowded with details. No factor could be left to chance, and he had to be completely confident in the duties he'd fulfill on-board the *Challenger*. No one wants to discover a crucial gap in their skills while carrying out a sensitive maneuver in orbit.

Ron never complained about the pace or the long weeks of absorbing information and practicing drills. He brought vigor and excitement to the final phase of training. His orderly mind and organized approach picked up new information quickly and then hungered for more. He wanted to have a hand in so many projects that there weren't enough hours in the day. Every aspect of the mission fascinated him. After others quit for the day and headed for bed, Ron was likely to still be at work if he was unsatisfied with his personal performance on some task. The other astronauts joked that maybe he was training to make the trip all alone.

Ron's duties on the shuttle had little to do with his specialized training in lasers. He performed seventeen experiments in a variety of fields. Some of his work would have medical research applications; he was expected to analyze cancer cells injected into laboratory rats. He would also study the physiological effects of zero gravity conditions on arthritis. Other experiments studied seed germination, cosmic ray physics, growth of spores, and protein crystallization. He played a major role in the RMS—the Remote Manipulator System—that used a mechanical arm to move objects in space.

Ron was also the official photographer and cinematographer for the mission, an ironic assignment since photography was one of the few areas that had never sparked any particular passion in him. Until that point, his photographic skills consisted of shouting, "Say cheese!" and then pressing the button on a point-and-shoot camera at birthdays and family gatherings. True to form, once Ron learned of his photographic duties on the upcoming shuttle flight, he immediately immersed himself in the subject, reading everything about photocomposition and camera operation that he could lay his hands on.

Several days before the launch date, NASA quarantined the astronauts to protect them from last-minute colds and viruses. A multi-million dollar mission couldn't grind to a halt because a crewmember contracted a head cold. Furthermore, in the close quarters of the shuttle, if one astronaut became ill the others would be seriously exposed to the same infection.

Launch authorities allowed family members to bid Ron and his fellow crewmembers goodbye, but kept thirty yards and a fence between us. On the night before the launch NASA personnel drove us to the launch pad to make our farewells. The spot-lighted shuttle stood majestically in the cool night, looming over us like a gigantic bird of prey yearning for the freedom of the distant sky. Standing in the presence of so much power was humbling. I caught myself holding my breath as I surveyed the steel curvature of the craft.

We shouted out words of encouragement to Ron and to other members of the *Challenger* crew. We had to yell a bit because of the conversational competition from the McNair Family and the other crew members' families. Sometimes we couldn't quite make out Ron's words, and he probably missed some of ours. Not that the words mattered much. Under the bravado and encouragement, love was the only message that night.

"We're proud of you."

"Take care of yourself."

"You all are in our prayers."

We felt anxious now that the time had come. Ron's wife,

Cheryl, wore a strong and confident face, but I wondered about her inner emotions. She was pregnant with their second child, Joy. I can only imagine the mix of pride, worry, and excitement that churned within her.

We repeatedly reminded one another that NASA had made a number of shuttle flights by now. They knew what they were doing. There was risk, of course, but some of the best minds in the world had planned and were overseeing this flight. NASA had an excellent safety record. A tragic fire during training had claimed the lives of Virgil Grissom, Edward White, and Roger Chaffee in 1967, but no American astronaut had ever been lost in flight. Ron would be fine. In a week he'd be back with us, after having made history.

Nearly half of Lake City turned out for the launch on the morning of February 3. Chartered buses practically transplanted the little South Carolina town to Florida. Spectators scattered and found the best vantage points available for the flight. NASA provided shuttle buses to transport families to a designated viewing area set aside for us. My parents and grandmother were there, as well as my aunts and my brother Eric. Dad beamed with pride and Mom fidgeted anxiously, glancing often at the sky. As the NASA shuttle bus stopped to unload us, my grandmother stood commandingly in the aisle and raised her hands.

"Let us pray," she said.

On the bus, every head bowed and every eye closed.

"*Oh God of our salvation,*" Grandmother said in a ringing voice, "*we're asking you today, to lay Your strong hand of blessing on Your child Ronald, and not just him, Lord, but on all five of these men going into space.*

Stand between them and every danger. Protect their lift-off and give them a safe homecoming. Your love reaches higher than the clouds, and we know that wherever Your children go, You are already there.

"When the flood came, You reached out and sealed the ark so no evil could enter that ship. Stretch out Your hand now and seal this spaceship. Wrap it up with Your mercy, and bring Your children back home again.

"As we wait on the ground, take the fear from our hearts. Wash away our doubts. Show us that You rule this world and every world. Fill us with Your peace—the peace of Christ that no one can steal.

We praise You for this clear weather and for this great day You've made. We thank You, for hearing this prayer and giving us what we ask. In the sweet name of our dear Lord and Savior Jesus Christ. Amen."

When she finished, a spirit of peace tempered our excitement. This was a powerful prayer, and when Grandmother said the Amen, we knew that everything would be all right.

The only family members not with us were Cheryl and Reggie. Spouses had a privileged spot inside one of the buildings, sheltered from the weather but with a clear and unobstructed view of the launch pad. I was glad that the pregnant mom was spared the chilly early morning air.

Over a public address system we heard the mission announcer commence the countdown. The original idea for counting backward before a rocket launch came from a 1929 German science-fiction movie by Fritz Lang. Regardless of its cinematic origin, I can't imagine a space launch without that respected ritual. As the numbers grew smaller I hugged my wife close and fixed my eyes on the shuttle. The huge spacecraft was exhaling white billows of gases and exhaust fumes as the mighty engines built power.

Right on schedule at 8:00 A.M. the countdown reached zero and explosions of flame raised the shuttle from the pad. The lift-off unleashed so much power that the earth quaked and the air trembled. I felt my insides shaking as the deafening roar grew almost unbearable. To an observer the shuttle appeared to lift slowly from the earth in the first moments of the launch.

Inside the craft the experience was altogether different.

Ron later told me, "At T minus zero I got a boot like I'd never felt. The vibrations simply shook every nut and bolt in the place. And that four million-pound vehicle literally lurched, leaped off the launch pad, and we were on our way."

My brother loved thrill-rides. I kidded that he had a need for speed. For instance, he only knew one way to snow ski—point the skis straight downhill and go full speed ahead; no traversing or slowing, just rocketing down the slope with every iota of velocity he could muster.

The shuttle launch was the ultimate roller coaster ride. Somewhere inside my poised, composed, scientifically detached brother was a little kid shouting, "Faster! Higher! Wow! That was great! Can we do it again?"

Ron spent the equivalent of eight days on the *Challenger*. Of course, earthly standards of night and day have little meaning for an orbiting space flight. Traveling at speeds in excess of 17,000 miles per hour, the *Challenger* circled the earth every ninety minutes. During their time in orbit, the crew lived with ninety minute "days", forty-five-minute periods of light, alternating with equal durations of darkness. From their own unique perspective, the astronauts spent 128 "days" orbiting the earth.

Mission Commander Vance Brand had been in space before on the *Columbia*, but the other four crewmen—pilot Robert Gibson, Robert Stewart, Bruce McCandless, and Ron—were rookies making their first foray into space. They experienced events and conditions on that flight that most of us can scarcely imagine.

At first, weightlessness was a strange feeling for Ron, but he soon found it to be great fun. In some of the films from the flight, my brother turned flips and clowned for the camera, revealing his delight in zero gravity. During sleep shifts, the astronauts strapped themselves into their bunks so they wouldn't bob around the interior of the craft. Ron later admitted to me that for a week after he returned to Earth, he slept clinging to his bed, afraid he'd float away in slumber.

Each astronaut acclimates to space conditions at his or her individual pace. Even after NASA's rigorous preparations, some space travelers experience a kind of nausea and vertigo called "space sickness." My brother had no such problems. Bruce McCandless said, "I think Ron adapted to space conditions faster than any of us."

Even in these novel circumstances, the crew went to work on their first day. Ron took charge of launching the communications satellite Westar 6 from the cargo bay. The deployment of the satellite proceeded flawlessly. Unfortunately, and through no fault of Ron's, the satellite's rocket boosters failed to fire properly and the satellite did not achieve its intended orbit. Sadly, the same problem developed with the other satellite released during *Challenger* Mission 41-B. The Indonesian satellite Palapa B-2 also ran afoul of a malfunctioning rocket engine.

These setbacks disappointed the crew, but subsequent shuttle missions recovered and repaired both satellites. In fact, Ron's work with the new Remote Manipulator Arm (RMA) paved the way for the later recovery efforts. The RMA is a fifty-foot, extendible arm that "grabs" errant satellites and brings them into the cargo bay for repair or return to earth.

Ron's long hours of simulator practice paid off when he used the Remote Manipulator Arm to position and hold Bruce McCandless in place during Extra-Vehicular Activity (EVA) in space. The manipulator arm provides a handy platform and workstation for an astronaut who needs to do EVA repairs or adjustments on the shuttle. Ron proved the value and practicality of the manipulator arm on that flight.

Mission 41-B broke new ground in yet another area. Stewart and McCandless took the first untethered space walks on that flight. I can scarcely imagine stepping into the void of space with no safety strap to keep me in touch with the spacecraft, but those brave men did just that. This marked the first use of the Manned Maneuvering Unit (MMU), a kind of jet pack that allowed the space walkers to move independently of the shuttle and return safely when their EVA work was completed. Stewart and McCandless spent nearly twelve hours outside the shuttle.

Perhaps Ron's most lasting contribution during the flight was his film record of the mission. Again, my brother found an occasion to clown around while carrying out serious work. During filming sessions he donned a black beret and a name tag identifying himself as "Cecil B. McNair." This was one of his humorous moments, but he was also paying homage to the late movie director, Cecil B. De Mille who filmed *The Ten Commandments*. Ron's videos and photographs provide a chronicle of Shuttle Mission 41-B. Planetariums across the country still use the footage Ron recorded on that flight. His shot of Bruce McCandless floating untethered in space is undoubtedly one of the best-known photos in the world. That image marvelously captures the courage, risk, and loneliness of the human quest to extend the boundaries of knowledge.

Taken as a whole, his camera work created a visual record of a remarkable moment in history, a film narrative that allows us earth-bound mortals to vicariously tread among the stars. No wonder Ron was later awarded a place in the prestigious American Society of Cinematographers.

What did Ron do when he wasn't busy with some task or experiment?

"I just looked out the window," he told me.

The panoramic view of Earth visible to him through the *Challenger* window endlessly fascinated him. He saw no national boundaries or dividing lines separating one people from another. Instead, the planet appeared as God intended, one intermeshing whole, an incredibly beautiful patchwork globe, diverse but unified.

"Truly there is no more beautiful sight," Ron said, "than to see the earth from space beyond. This planet is an exquisite oasis. Warmth emanates from the earth when you look at her from space... My wish is that we would allow this planet to be the beautiful oasis that she is, and allow ourselves to live more in the peace that she generates."

Many astronauts have spoken of a spiritual awakening when confronted by the infinite grandeur of outer space. A news reporter once asked Ron about that aspect of space flight.

"Did you feel any closer to God?" He inquired.

Ron's reply was characteristically matter-of-fact.

"Being in space was not any different from being on earth, from a spiritual perspective," he said.

"No great awakening?" The reporter pressed on.

"I left earth believing in God, and I came back still believing," he said. "Maybe if a person went into space without any faith, the beauty of earth might awaken a spiritual inclination."

With a shrug he added, "That didn't apply to me. I know God's with me wherever I go."

My brother achieved one more very personal first while orbiting on the *Challenger*. Ron brought a saxophone with him on the flight and played the first musical solo in space.

This may sound like a simple undertaking for an accomplished musician like Ron, but nothing could be further from the truth. Playing in space confronted him with tough challenges and perplexing choices. For instance, he wrestled with what variety of saxophone to take on board the shuttle. Normally Ron played the tenor sax, but space in his stowaway on the shuttle was extremely limited. A tenor wouldn't fit. Neither would a straight soprano. The choice had to be a curved soprano sax.

Working with Kurt Heisig, a musician and saxophone craftsman in California, Ron tried to anticipate the problems of playing in space. Low cabin pressure would make the sax much harder to play, and Ron worked on exercises, experimented with different reeds, and strengthened his wind to compensate for that obstacle. The low humidity of the cabin air also presented a problem, causing the pads to dry out. Also, the absence of gravity caused globules of moisture to form within the saxophone and distort the music causing a bubbling sound.

At the last minute NASA gave formal permission for Ron to take his sax into space. He did indeed play there to a captive audience of his fellow astronauts. He opened with "What the World Needs Now Is Love, Sweet Love" and followed it with "Reach Out and Touch Somebody's Hand." Ron chose those songs to express his hopes for a world filled with love, a unified planet in which people near and far accept each other as neighbors.

Knowing how much emotion Ron poured into his music, I suspect that the music he played in orbit was his prayer for the healing of a divided and fearful Earth. From the lofty perspective of the *Challenger*, Ron glimpsed the nations as perhaps God sees them and caught a vision of what the world could become if only we lived as brothers and sisters.

The crew of Mission 41-B clapped and cheered when the last saxophone notes faded away. The on-the-spot reviews were predictably full of good humor and bad puns.

"Out of this world!"

"A stellar performance, Ron. Just heavenly."

"Those are the highest notes I've ever heard on the sax."

"You're the best jazz saxophone player out of the world."

Unfortunately, back here on planet Earth we didn't get to hear the performance. For some reason Ron's music was caught in a news blackout. He did record the performance for posterity, but, in a stroke of terrible luck, someone accidentally taped over that cassette and lost Ron's music. Sometime later, NASA released a photo of Ron playing the saxophone in space. He had chosen his songs "What the World Needs Now..." and "Reach Out and Touch..."carefully to convey a message of love to the world. However, his musical event never reached the people of the world as he'd hoped. That may have been his greatest disappointment after Shuttle Mission 41-B.

Ron had big plans for a live-broadcast performance of the saxophone on his next shuttle flight. After some wheeling and dealing, he received NASA's permission to take the sax into space again so that he could play a tribute to the sesquicentennial celebration of Texas, a fitting contribution from the Johnson Space Center at Houston. The composer Jean-Michael Jarre had composed a jazz piece specifically for Ron's outer space performance. He'd hoped to record it for a commercial release as the first song debuted in space.

Regrettably, that live saxophone performance never took place. I am eternally thankful that Ron could carry his beloved music into space, bringing together two of the great passions of his life. I wish I could have heard those songs coaxed from a contrary saxophone in a dry, low-pressure cabin in zero gravity. He poured himself into his music, and I'm sure that was as true in space as on Earth. I grieve the loss of that tape, and I will always mourn the music left unplayed when he died.

CHAPTER 13

———

Down To Earth

Early the morning of February 11, the cheery voice of mission control crackled over *Challenger*'s radio.

"*Challenger*, be apprised that you are approaching the point of re-entry. You may begin descent procedure at your discretion."

"Copy," replied Commander Vance Brand.

"Come on home, boys, and Godspeed."

Roughly halfway around the world from their landing destination, Commander Brand initiated the descent protocol. The manner of its return to earth would signify one final first accomplished on Shuttle Mission 41-B. The whole point of the shuttle program was to find a way to re-use most of the spacecraft and to return the vessel to Earth in a practical and economical manner. Prior to Ron's flight, the shuttles landed in California near Edwards Air Force Base, where there is a large, dry lakebed that NASA pressed into service as a landing area. The lakebed was flat and offered plenty of room—and therefore a healthy margin of error—for returning shuttles.

A large landing area was important. NASA's pilots reported that the stubby-bodied shuttles were challenging to fly during their re-entry to Earth's atmosphere. In fact, some said that the shuttle "handled like a brick" or "flew like a plank." NASA's engineers expected such comments. The shape of the shuttle was a worst-of-both-worlds compromise simultaneously accommodating rocket-style launches and airplane-like landings. The end result was a hybrid craft with more resistance than a typical rocket and less aerodynamic lift than an airplane.

Landing in the lakebed in California was a prudent precaution while the first shuttle pilots learned to handle the awkward flyer. After the shuttle landed safely, a jumbo 747 jet piggybacked the orbiter cross-country to Florida in preparation for the next lift-off. This arrangement meant extra expense for transporting the shuttle across the continent and also resulted in wasted time between space flights. Since the shuttle program was intended to generate income, NASA wanted to eliminate needless costs and cut down the time between flights.

The logical way to accomplish these goals was to land the returning shuttles near Kennedy Space Center instead of in California. Ron's shuttle mission was the first to return directly to Florida from outer space. NASA had designed a long and rather narrow landing strip on a finger of land surrounded by marshy water. Landing safely on the strip demanded far greater precision than bringing the shuttle to ground safely in the sprawling California lakebed.

The drama of *Challenger*'s return from orbit began long

before the craft actually approached the Florida landing area. While in orbit the craft had flown upside-down and nose-first. Brand ordered the firing of the forward thrusters to turn the shuttle into a tail-first position. Then the more powerful rear thrusters fired to slow the orbiter's forward speed. After twenty-five minutes the rocket thrusters sufficiently diminished the *Challenger's* 17,500 miles per hour velocity to begin the fall from orbit. During that process, the crew again fired the forward thrusters to turn the *Challenger* belly-down and nose-first. As the final step toward re-entry, Brand burned the leftover fuel in the forward thrusters. The forward portion of the orbiter encounters the highest heat during re-entry, and any remaining fuel might pose a fire hazard.

From this point, the shuttle descended in a controlled fall from low earth orbit. The orbiter picked up speed as it plunged toward the earth. The carefully calculated angle of descent used atmospheric resistance to slow the craft. By way of comparison, consider what happens when a swimmer leaps off the high-dive. Entering the water slows the diver's descent so that the swimmer doesn't smash into the concrete floor of the pool. In the same way, the *Challenger* relied on the atmosphere to slow the descent and save the ship from crashing.

As the shuttle hurtled downward, air resistance generated heat on the skin of the spaceship. Friction is a potentially deadly enemy for returning space flights. When we briskly rub our hands together on a cold day, we welcome the warmth created by the friction of skin against skin. On the *Challenger* the friction of air molecules rubbing against the hull resulted in more than pleasant warmth.

The on-board computer system struck a careful balance

as the *Challenger* angled toward earth. On one hand, too shallow a descent wouldn't slow the ship sufficiently for a safe landing. On the other hand, if the *Challenger* fell too steeply the excessive friction heat would incinerate the ship.

Anyone who glances up at a shooting star on a clear summer night will see atmospheric friction at work. Thousands of meteors bombard our planet every day. Friction is the reason those hurtling stones don't batter our cities and blast our neighborhoods. Meteors nearly always burn up long before reaching the surface of the earth. The atmosphere that enwraps our world is a highly efficient natural defense system protecting us from falling debris.

Unfortunately, Mother Nature can't tell the difference between a falling space rock and a landing spaceship. As the *Challenger* pushed deeper into the atmosphere, the shuttle became a plummeting ball of flame glowing a brilliant cherry red. The crew inside the craft could see the hail of sparks reflected through the windows. The crimson glare painted the interior of the *Challenger* a somber red.

The ship survived the super-heated re-entry thanks to an elaborate, multi-layered insulation system using felt blankets, ceramic blankets, ceramic tiles, and carbon-carbon leading edge. These materials have different levels of tolerance, and the most resistant are placed on those areas that generate the highest heat.

At maximum temperature, the *Challenger* reached 3,000 degrees Fahrenheit. At that point, the *Challenger* experienced the anticipated "ionization blackout." Super-heated ionized gases surrounding the vessel blocked radio communication with ground control. For twelve minutes, the *Challenger* crew was cut off from the world.

Once the *Challenger* actually re-entered earth's atmosphere, the craft began flying in much the same manner as an airplane, and the relatively small delta wings in the rear allowed the orbiter to glide toward earth in a series of long, S-shaped curves. These banking turns lowered the *Challenger's* speed still more. At 140 miles away, the *Challenger* picked up the radio message from the beacon at the runway.

So far, the descent path was computer-guided, but at twenty-five miles out, Commander Vance Brand took manual control for the final landing approach. Brand carefully calculated position, angle of descent, and speed for the monstrous glider. The *Challenger* was an unpowered vehicle, and if Brand fell short of the runway or overshot the landing area, he could not regain altitude for a second pass. If the shuttle was incorrectly positioned on its first landing attempt, Brand would not get a second chance.

The pilot steered the orbiter into a spiral descent to decrease altitude and adjust the direction of approach to the runway. In the final landing procedure, Brand pointed the *Challenger's* nose sharply downward in a heart-freezing descent seven times steeper than that of a commercial airplane. The landing strip stretched down a skinny neck of land with alligator-infested water on both sides.

"Looks like those alligators might be ready for breakfast," Ron commented. "I hope Vance keeps us on the straight and narrow."

At 2,000 feet above the strip, Brand yanked the nose upward to slow the descent and deployed the landing gear.

With an abrupt thump the *Challenger* touched down at 200 miles per hour. Immediately Commander Brand braked the craft and released the parachute from the tail. The rapid deceleration jolted the crewmembers forward, pressing the restraining straps tightly against their chests.

Halfway down the landing strip, the *Challenger* lumbered to a halt as the cabin rang with cheers, whistles, and congratulations. After eight days in space and 128 orbits of Earth the far-traveling *Challenger* squatted safely on *terra firma*. Ron was home, and Shuttle Mission 41-B was history.

CHAPTER 14

———

A Hero's Welcome

Experienced pilots claim that any landing the passengers can walk away from is a good landing. Brand and Gibson had guided the *Challenger* to a good landing, but the crew had trouble walking away. They'd been in space for over 190 hours. Eight days may seem a brief vacation from gravity, but in that short time the muscles of the astronauts had noticeably atrophied. Even though they'd exercised in orbit using resistance machines, the absence of gravity had physically weakened them. The returning heroes could barely muster the strength to unstrap themselves and rise from their seats.

"I was looking forward to a big breakfast," Ron said as he struggled to stand, "but I guess I've gained some weight since I left."

"Yeah, about a thousand pounds," lamented Bruce McCandless.

Ron later tried to describe to me how he felt when he first landed."

"Remember how it felt in football practice after a really hard workout?" he asked. "You know, after we'd pushed that tackle dummy up and down the field for an hour. By the time Coach let us go home, our legs were wobbling. We could hardly lift our arms. That's how I felt when we landed."

"You were exhausted," I said.

"Not really," Ron said. "I felt energized, as if I'd just stepped off the world's best roller coaster."

"But your limbs didn't want to move, like you were in molasses, huh?"

"Right," Ron said. "Imagine waking up one morning feeling great, ready to tackle the world. But when you try to get out of bed, you discover someone has tied concrete blocks to your arms and legs."

Sluggish heaviness is a common experience for returning astronauts, the apparently inevitable cost of shaking off the shackles of gravity. I once met a Russian cosmonaut who'd spent over 300 days in space. After his return to earth he was bed-ridden for nearly a month while he acclimated anew to the tug of gravity. The *Challenger* crew spent half an hour in the craft stretching and limbering strength back into lazy muscles before they dared descend the ladder to solid ground.

An enthusiastic nation was eager to welcome them home. Ron and his shuttle comrades became instant heroes. One particular event stands out for me as proof of my brother's celebrity status. I called my mother that day with the big news.

"Mom, you'll never guess what I'm holding in my hand

right now," I teased her.

"Don't you think you're getting a little old for guessing games?"

"I'm holding a magazine," I told her. "Guess which one."

"I don't know," she huffed. "*Time?*"

"Nope. Bigger than *Time*. This is the magazine for African-Americans, the national news for black folks."

"Okay," she said. "You're holding a *Jet* magazine."

"Not just any issue of *Jet*, Mom. The latest issue just now hitting the stands. And who do you think is on the cover?"

I heard her suck in a sudden breath.

"No!" she said.

"Yes!" I told her. "Ron—your Number Two Son—has his ugly face plastered all over the front of *Jet!*"

"Good Lord!" she squealed. "Get off the phone. I have to call the drugstore and see if they've got a copy."

That day I knew my brother had ascended into the ranks of greatness. The shuttle flight was high, but *Jet* was higher. I took that cover to a photo shop and had it enlarged so I could mat and frame it. The enlarged cover hangs on my wall to this day. Among my favorite pictures, Ron's *Jet* cover ranks a close second to our group graduation snapshot.

Articles, interviews, speeches, and honorary awards filled the next several months of Ron's life. He dined with celebrities and hobnobbed with politicians, but fame never puffed up his opinion of himself. He accepted the accolades with both grace and a grain of salt. Ron honestly believed he was nothing special. At every opportunity, he offered himself as an example of what determination can accomplish.

"Anyone can do what I've done," he told students. "If you are willing to apply yourself and work hard, you can achieve even more than I have. If you will commit yourself to your dreams, you can go as high as you like. Take my word for it: the sky is not the limit."

Although Ron played down the scope of his achievement, he profoundly appreciated the outpouring of acclaim and affection that attended his return from space. Our alma mater, A & T, honored him in a moving award ceremony. When he rose to address the full-house crowd of students, faculty, and alumni, pride and gratitude shone in his eyes.

"To go around the world 128 times at 17,500 miles per hour aboard the Rolls-Royce of space flight is one experience," he said. "But to come home amidst warmth and appreciation is an experience of equal magnitude."

The high point for Ron was the welcome parade that awaited him back in our hometown of Lake City. In the eyes of the world, that homecoming was the least of his honors, but to my brother the cheers of former teachers, schoolmates, and neighbors meant much more than his gold astronaut pin or his conversations with President Ronald Reagan. This was Ron's home and these were his people. His heart still lived in Lake City, and the praise of these old friends was the pinnacle of success.

The town turned out to applaud our local hero. The mayor declared that the date of my brother's homecoming would be officially designated Ronald McNair Day. blacks and whites stood side-by-side, lining the highway along the parade route. No throng so large had ever before assembled in Lake City to honor any person, much less a black man. But we'd never before had a homegrown astronaut. This was the first time a space traveler had graced our streets.

The parade procession moved along what had formerly been Highway 52. Now that four-lane stretch running through the heart of town was renamed Ron McNair Boulevard. My brother served as the Grand Marshall of his own homecoming celebration. He rode in the lead parade car, an open convertible, and waved happily to the crowd. He shouted greetings to old friends and called out familiar names. Streamers unfurled and draped across the convertible. Balloons bobbed in the air, batted by continual shouts and cheers. Adding to the joyous tumult, our high school band marched behind Ron's car. The band in which he and I had once played blared exuberant tunes while majorettes high-stepped with pride. Ron's smile grew brighter when he saw blacks and whites marching together in the band of our formerly segregated high school.

My parents also rode along in the parade, basking in reflected glory. They tried to remain suitably humble, but failed miserably. Their son, the astronaut, was the hero of the day. This was the boy they had birthed, fed, raised, and sent through school. My brother's national fame didn't belong solely to him. The McNair family owned a share in that recognition, as did the whole black community in Lake City. Ron was the living, smiling truth of what our people could accomplish. The black astronaut rolling into Lake City on the cheers of the crowd symbolized what African-Americans could become.

Grandmother's wise eyes glimmered with tears when she reflected on the jubilant celebration.

"Who would have believed such a day would come?" she asked in wonder. "All those people shouting and cheering for one of our own."

I knew by "one of our own" she meant not only our family, but also our race.

"A street named after Ron. The mayor shaking his hand. His story in the county paper," she said. She shook her gray head slowly, as if afraid she might awake from a heavenly dream.

"Yes, Grandmother," I said. "The world is changing. Things are getting better."

"God is so good," she said. "Now I know how old Simeon felt when he first saw baby Jesus. 'O Lord, now let your servant depart in peace according to Your word, for my eyes have seen Your salvation.'"

I patted her hand and said, "Grandmother, you're not going anywhere."

"I'm not ready to go, either," she assured me, "not while the party's going on and there's more cake to eat."

Whenever Ron made a visit to Lake City, he stopped by our old high school. Like Mom and Grandmother, he was an energetic advocate for education. He loved visiting classrooms and conversing with students. Many of our former teachers were still at the school and they eagerly encouraged his visits. Lesson plans were tabled when Ron McNair walked through the door.

In the midst of Ron's outer space stories and examples of applied science, some student invariably asked, "How did you do it?" The wording of the question varied, but the intent was plain. How did a local boy become world-famous? How did he learn so much from tattered textbooks in a small-town school on the wrong side of the tracks? How did he make the million-mile journey from the tobacco fields to the space shuttle?

That question was Ron's cue to jump into what I jokingly called his *You-Can-Do-It* sermon. Like many sermons I've heard, this one had three points.

"You know how I feel about education," Ron told the kids. "Education is the step-ladder that allows you to climb to new heights. The more you learn the farther you can ascend. If you are happy cropping tobacco and picking cotton, you can drop out of school right now. Anybody here want to spend the rest of your life in the fields?"

Nobody raised a hand.

"No?" Ron feigned surprise. "Picking cotton is great fun, especially after your hands start bleeding."

Laughter and a few knowing smiles.

"Do any of you want to be a teacher? A doctor? An engineer? An astronaut?"

Hands flew up for each career.

"Then stay in school," Ron admonished them. "But just showing up for class isn't nearly enough. To get the most out of school and make the most of my learning experiences, I've cultivated three personality traits. These three habits have served me well, and they'll work for you, too."

The students leaned forward to catch every word. Ron raised his index finger and said, "Number One is discipline. I know what you're thinking. 'Discipline is what my parents and teachers do to me when I act up.' That's one form of discipline, but the best discipline is the kind you apply to yourself. Instead of waiting for someone else to push you in the right direction, push yourself. Decide where you want to go, what you need to do to get there, and then make yourself do it. Stay motivated and follow through.

"Do you think I enjoyed working through the night in the lab at MIT? I didn't. Sometimes I'd lay my head down on the worktable for a five-minute rest and wake up two hours later with a blazing headache and crick in my neck. There's nothing fun about lab work at three in the morning. Do you know what kept me there? Discipline. When I was about your age I decided I wanted a Ph.D. Even when it was hard and I was exhausted, I did whatever I had to do to become Dr. McNair. Discipline got me through."

He raised two fingers and flashed them at the class.

"Character Trait Number Two is what I call hanging it over the edge."

That elicited giggles from the boys. Ron smiled and pressed on.

"I learned about hanging it over the edge from the California surfers who stick out one foot over the front of the board. Mountain climbers use the same phrase. Anybody can walk up to the edge, but only someone with determination can go another couple of inches and hang it over the edge. Don't be afraid of uncertainty. Take risks. Every time you face what you fear, you come away stronger. I'm not encouraging you to be foolhardy or reckless. But if you want to reach the mountaintop, you'll have to take a few chances to get there."

Three fingers.

"The third character trait that got me into space is the rejection of worry. If you're lying awake at night worrying about your problems, you're wasting energy. If it's a problem you can attack, do it. Worry won't make that problem go away, but you might. Or if the problem is out of your hands, forget it and move on. You'll do no good worrying about things outside your control.

"Do you have any idea how many things can go wrong on a space flight? Thousands of accidents are possible on a mission as complex as sending people into space. I decided not to worry about that while I was up there. I had my job to do, and I did my part as well as I could. Which was the best way to spend that week in space? Chewing my fingernails and watching for meteorites? Or floating upside down and enjoying the ride?"

One of the boys shouted, "Upside-down and hanging it over the edge!"

Ron laughed and the class joined in.

"Discipline, hanging it over the edge, and refusing to worry," Ron concluded. "That's how I did it, and that's how you can do it, too. Cultivate those three traits and you can go anywhere you want in this world—or even out of this world."

By the time he finished, those kids had begun to dream. I saw it in their eyes and read it in their thoughtful expressions. I also recognized the satisfaction Ron found in speeches like that.

Inspiring others was one of his continuing dreams, especially when he connected with economically disadvantaged kids. He remembered where he came from and loved encouraging the youngsters who were still there.

In spite of his inspirational talks, at least one member of our family thought Ron should say more. A few days after the parade, Grandmother pointedly suggested that her grandson wasn't communicating enough about the most important things in life. When Ron dropped in to visit our grandparents, Grandmother patted the worn cushion on the slip-covered sofa.

"Sit here with me," she invited.

When Ron settled beside her, she half-turned to meet his eyes.

"Uh-oh," he said. "This is the look I used to get when I was in trouble. What have I done?"

"It's nothing you've done," Grandmother said. "It's what you haven't done. You've been back here in Lake City for three days now, and not once have I heard you mention the name of Jesus."

Grandmother laid her callused hand on his.

"You've been up in space and you've had big fun," she went on. "You know, I'm so proud of you I could bust. But you're back home now, and you've got the chance to tell people about your Lord. People are listening to you, but you aren't telling them what they need to hear."

With his free hand, Ron reached out and smoothed a stray strand of gray hair.

"You're right, Grandmother," he admitted. "I haven't shared much about my faith, not yet. But you know I wouldn't have set one foot inside that space shuttle if Jesus wasn't there first."

Ron took that conversation to heart, and he often related Grandmother's words in his speeches. The story of his chat with Grandmother offered him a way to talk about his faith even in secular settings.

"I don't profess to be a preacher," Ron told his listeners, "but I am a Christian. I know God has a strange way of using anything or anybody to convey His message. I may be the most inept ambassador He has ever spoken through, but I believe God can use even me."

I heard Ron tell that story so many times, I decided to share it with others, too. In 2004, MIT invited me to visit the campus and participate in the Black Alumni of MIT (BAMIT) 25th Anniversary Celebration & Gala in which they honored my brother. When I spoke that evening, I recalled aloud the importance of Ron's faith. I recounted the talk he had with Grandmother, a story he'd told so often in so many places. When the Gala was coming to a close, an MIT alumnus sought me out. Taking my arm, he led me to a quiet corner and spoke earnestly about his memory of Ron.

"I was a student here when your brother spoke on campus," he told me. "I didn't know Ron personally. I enrolled at MIT after he graduated. Everybody was buzzing about the astronaut coming to campus, so I decided to go hear his speech."

The alum looked over my shoulder as if gazing into the past.

"I didn't expect much," he admitted. "The usual nose-to-the-grindstone pep talk. Honestly, I don't remember a word from the first twenty minutes of Ron's talk. But when he talked about his grandmother—the same story you repeated tonight—that caught my attention. I was a hard-nosed scientist in those days. I didn't accept anything that couldn't be squeezed into a test tube or spread on a microscope slide. I didn't need God because I already had life figured out."

He fell silent for a moment, still staring into the distance, and a tiny smile played across his lips.

He turned his gaze back to me and said, "Ronald McNair changed my life. Here was this laser physicist, a scientist on the cutting edge, and he's talking about his faith in God. I couldn't get those words out of my head: 'I wouldn't have set one foot inside that space shuttle if Jesus wasn't there first.'"

He smiled openly at me and squeezed my arm.

"Before that week ended, I gave my life to Christ," he said. "I never got to tell your brother. But I thought I would tell you."

"Thank you for sharing that with me," I said. "Ron would be proud that his words helped you find your way to God. I wish he had known about this."

"Maybe he does know," the man said.

We shook hands and he disappeared into the crowd.

In Ron's mind, no conflict separated science from faith. Knowledge is one way of seeing the world; faith is another. He refused to pass through this rich and beautiful life squinting through one eye when he could explore reality with both eyes open. The Creator whose natural laws form the basis of science is also the Savior whose love is the foundation of religion.

Just as Ron loved instructing others in the basics of physics, he also found satisfaction in sharing his understanding of God's saving love. He talked openly about his beliefs, not only in Sunday School, but in classrooms and lecture halls. Wherever he found himself, he laid his faith out for all to see.

My brother and I grew up in farming country. Ron knew that no harvest comes unless the seeds are first sown. He sowed his faith and left the results in God's hands. He may not have seen evidence of his sowing, but Ron, man of the Spirit, and scientist, had no difficulty believing in the unseen.

CHAPTER 15

——

One More Flight

"**I** won't stay at NASA forever," Ron told me, "but I'd like to get another flight under my belt before I try my hand at something new."

Ron and I kept in touch in spite of the miles between Houston and Atlanta. Sometimes he called from home, but today he was phoning from a hotel room on the final leg of a NASA public relations tour.

"After you've been an astronaut," I asked him, "where do you go but down?"

He laughed.

"In outer space I discovered there is no up or down," he lectured me. "There's only motion, and I'm almost ready to get moving again."

I sipped my soft drink and waited. I knew he was leading up to something.

"Some of my friends think I ought to run for office," he said casually. "Maybe ride the astronaut express into Congress."

"It worked for John Glenn," I said. "Are you serious about this?"

"Just trying it on for size," he said. "I'm not sure if it's a good fit. I've never considered myself much of politician."

We both laughed.

"Politicians do make a difference in the world," I said.

"So do educators," Ron said. "I've put out some feelers at a couple of universities."

Ron was a natural teacher. He came alive in front of a classroom. His enthusiasm for learning drew students to him like orbiting satellites. I knew teaching at a university was a good direction for Ron and I told him so.

"Yeah, it feels right," he agreed. "But I do want one more shuttle flight before I leave."

"You gotta have one more roller coaster ride," I kidded.

"There's nothing else like a shuttle launch," Ron said. "I've never felt such a adrenaline rush as I did when those main engines fired up."

Ron had spoken about this so fervently that I almost felt as if I'd had the experience myself. After his first shuttle flight, he shared with me a couple of videotapes from his mission. I enjoyed the onboard footage of everyday life in space, but Ron loved the video footage depicting the lift-off. He watched it endlessly, rewinding it over and over like a child replaying a favorite cartoon. He turned the volume up to full power, shoved the bass over to max, and sat entranced as the

TV screen replayed the explosive ignition. My living room floorboards rumbled with the thunder of the rocket engines. Eventually, he blew out my brand new speakers.

He longed to relive that experience, but the videotape was a pale imitation. Ron yearned to ride the shuttle again, harness that unimaginable power and hurl himself into space faster than the speed of sound. I could feel his excitement.

"One more flight," he said over the phone.

Only a few weeks after that conversation, NASA selected Ron to fly his second mission on the *Challenger*. The launch was scheduled for July 1985. Although his mind was already looking beyond NASA, he was excited about Mission 51-L. The announcement of another flight so soon allayed his concerns that a long wait laid before him.

In fact, the wait turned out to be longer than anyone expected. NASA changed the projected payload for 51-L several times in the following months, and those revisions postponed the launch repeatedly. Shifts in mission goals are typical, especially during the early planning stages, so payload changes weren't unusual. With so many unresolved payload decisions, mission planners re-scheduled the July flight for January 22, 1986.

Had that been the final launch date, Ron and his crew would probably be alive today; however, other factors further complicated the matter. *Challenger's* sister ship, the *Columbia*, sat poised on the launch pad on December 19, all systems cleared for launch shortly before 8:00 A.M. Fourteen seconds prior to engine ignition, on-board computers signaled a problem with the nozzle assembly of the right-side solid-rocket booster. The countdown reverted to T-minus twenty minutes while technicians examined the malfunction. The tech crew decided to replace the faulty mechanism, a choice that scrubbed that day's flight. The launch date moved to January 4, and then to January 6 so that NASA employees could enjoy an extended Christmas vacation. In conjunction with those decisions, *Challenger's* launch was bumped to January 23, and then January 24, both to accommodate the *Columbia* and to provide additional training time for Ron and his crewmates.

On January 6, the launch team again halted *Columbia's* countdown, this time due to a problem in the liquid-fuel propulsion system. Bad weather prevented the launch the next day; a fuel line problem aborted another attempted launch on January 9. By now the luckless *Columbia* crew wondered if their shuttle would ever get off the pad. On January 10, storms and heavy rain grounded another launch. The *Columbia* finally launched on January 12, twenty-four days late.

Meanwhile, NASA again postponed *Challenger* Mission 51-L, moving the launch to January 25. The crew planned to fly to Kennedy Space Center on January 22 to make final preparations for their flight, but bad weather in Senegal (Africa) delayed their flight. In Dakar, Senegal, there is an emergency landing area available for the shuttle in case of problems in the later portion of the ascent toward space. A transatlantic landing was one of several emergency scenarios sketched by NASA for systems failure during launch. Depending upon the altitude of the shuttle if trouble arose, the commander might attempt either the Senegal landing or RTLS (return to launch site). Achieving a lower-than-planned earth orbit presented a third possibility.

NASA formulated these emergency options in order to deal with engine or instrument failure. In every case, the failsafe plans assume that the crew would remain within the shuttle. No escape program existed for removing the astronauts from the ship. Early in the program, the *Columbia* carried two ejector seats. Other shuttles never received similar equipment because of technical and feasibility issues. The ejector seats were later removed from the *Columbia*. If problems arose after launch, the safety of the crew required the rescue of the entire shuttle.

The sandstorms and reduced visibility in Dakar eliminated one of the emergency escape plans. Accordingly, NASA put the launch on hold until the weather cleared in Senegal. The astronauts spent another night in Houston, and then flew to Kennedy Space Center one day later for a launch that had been bumped from Saturday to Sunday.

Again, unexpected difficulties dogged *Challenger's* departure. Meteorologists reported a cold front moving in from Texas. They predicted cloud cover, rain, and fog for Sunday. At 10:00 Saturday night, mission planners moved the launch date to Monday. Ironically, the weather predictions were wrong. The Texas cold front moved more slowly than anticipated, and the shuttle could have launched without problems on Sunday.

The astronauts rose early on Monday, enjoyed the traditional steak-and-eggs breakfast, and arrived at the shuttle at around 7:00. As the ground control crew greeted the fliers, one technician donned an academic mortarboard in deference to Christa McAuliffe. The teacher beamed at the tomfoolery, obviously pleased by the recognition. McAuliffe was the media darling of Mission 51-L. A civilian without technical training, she represented the first "ordinary" person to blast off for outer space. From orbit she would teach two televised lessons to students around the world. She joked to reporters that no teacher had ever been better prepared.

"I've worked on these lessons since September," she said. "I hope everybody tunes in. I want a big classroom."

Along with Ron and Christa McAuliffe, five more members comprised the crew.

Dick Scobee, a veteran of space flight, was mission commander, and his pilot was Michael Smith. Like Scobee, Smith was a former test pilot. Unlike the Commander, this was Smith's first space flight.

Mission Specialist Judy Resnik was an electrical engineer from Akron, Ohio. Her maiden flight on the *Discovery* made her the second American woman in space.

Mission Specialist Ellison Onizuka was a Japanese-American from Hawaii. He had earned his gold astronaut pin on the *Discovery* and hoped to spend many years flying for NASA. For this avid outdoorsman, space flight was the ultimate adventure.

Payload Specialist Gregory Jarvis would fly on the *Challenger* as an employee of Hughes Aircraft Corporation. Twice before Jarvis had been bumped from shuttle flights, and he was exuberant at having finally won a berth on the *Challenger*.

Along with the limelight accompanying the first teacher in space, Mission 51-L could claim other distinctions. Halley's comet was making a once-every-seventy-years transit and *Challenger* intended to make the intimate acquaintance of the nomad before the comet disappeared for another seven decades. The fleeting presence of Halley's comet put pressure on NASA to get the *Challenger* off the ground as soon as possible. The shuttle would also carry aloft a satellite necessary to complete an around-the-world communications system. This, too, was time-sensitive.

Mission 51-L represented one of NASA's most ambitions projects. The total payload on this flight weighed in at more than twenty-four tons, the heaviest ever launched. Even more than earlier launches, this mission proved that space flight could be profitable and self-sustaining. In every sense, NASA had a great deal riding on the *Challenger*.

By 8:00 a.m. the seven astronauts had donned helmets, entered the craft, and strapped in for the launch. After the fliers were aboard, mission technicians closed the shuttle hatch, but computer monitors did not confirm that the hatch was properly secured.

Commander Scobee told launch control, "We'd like to have one of the guys who's very familiar with the latches to come inside, close the door, check them to make sure they're all okay."

Mechanical engineers checked the hatch, quickly repaired a minor microswitch problem, but then ran into trouble with a stuck bolt. When the repair crew failed to budge the bolt, they decided to drill it out. A hand drill brought for that purpose had dead batteries. A worker fetched fresh batteries, but the drill couldn't do the job. A technician finally cut off the bolt with a hacksaw.

By this time, cloud cover had rolled over Cape Canaveral.

High winds buffeted the landing strip where the *Challenger* would make an emergency landing if problems developed in the first few minutes of the flight. The windy conditions might also cause trouble for the launch itself since the shuttle carried such a heavy payload. Furthermore, the lift-off had been delayed so long that flight controllers needed to reprogram the navigational computers to compensate for the earth's movement.

At 12:36 P.M. a NASA spokesman announced, "We are going to scrub for today."

After spending more than five hours strapped into their seats, the disappointed astronauts exited the shuttle. The crowd of spectators, including many members of my family, drifted away to homes and hotel rooms at the end of the anti-climactic vigil.

By this time, I, Dad, Mom, Eric, and our families had been in Florida several days. We arrived on Saturday for a Sunday launch. Now on Monday afternoon, we'd waited through two aborts. NASA rescheduled for Tuesday morning, January 28. The weather was still uncertain, and I feared more delays were likely. We wanted to support Ron, but my wife Mary was pregnant, and her health and comfort were foremost in my mind. Ron called to inform us that the shuttle launch would probably be postponed again. If that happened, the shuttle fuel tanks would have to be drained and refueled—and this process could take a couple of days. After a brief family conference, we reluctantly decided to return to our homes in Atlanta. My mother stayed behind for the launch, but the rest of us hit the road after wishing Ron good luck.

That night, the Cape experienced a record-breaking chill.

Temperatures fell well below freezing, and engineers fretted over the possible detrimental effects of the icy conditions. Through the night, workers took measures to prevent freeze-ups in launch pad waterlines. A far more critical issue sparked a debate about the safety of the solid-rocket boosters.

The solid-rocket boosters are manufactured in four sections, and the joint between each segment is sealed with a rubber O-ring. Engineers from Morton Thiokol, the manufacturer of the engines, recommended postponing the flight until the weather warmed. Ideally, the spongy O-rings flexed to maintain an airtight seal, but the intense cold might prevent them from seating properly. Examination of O-rings after other cold weather flights showed blackened areas where gases had seeped through the seal; those flights had launched in temperatures in the low sixties, not nearly as cold as the weather projected for *Challenger's* lift-off. If the O-rings failed, hot gases could escape from the joints like a 6000-degree torch. The potential danger was "burn through," leading to a fiery engine explosion.

Managers at Marshall Space Flight Center in Huntsville, Alabama, argued that the Morton Thiokol engineers didn't have enough data to support their disaster scenario. Since Marshall Space Flight Center is the arm of NASA in charge of the solid-rocket booster program, its opinion carries weight. After some debate, the Morton Thiokol engineers bowed to pressure and sent a message to the Kennedy Space Center approving the Tuesday morning launch. Executive personnel at Launch Control had no knowledge of the disagreement.

Probably no one involved in the debate noted an ominous coincidence. Nineteen years prior to the crucial O-ring discussion—to the day—three astronauts had died in flames during a training drill while sealed in a command module. In the aftermath of the Apollo fire, NASA instituted rigorous safety standards. Many in the agency felt that those standards had grown looser in recent years.

The argument over the O-rings represented a change in the mentality of the space program. Instead of the Marshall Space Flight Center personnel having to prove that the intended flight was safe, the Morton Thiokol engineers were expected to prove it wasn't. Instead of saying, "We won't fly unless we know it's safe," some NASA officials adopted the position: "We're going to fly unless there's proof we shouldn't."

The philosophical shift was subtle; the results were not.

CHAPTER 16

———

Go With Throttle Up!

Through the night, nervous technicians monitored the build-up of ice on the launch pad as the wind chill hit ten degrees below zero. A technical glitch unrelated to the freezing temperatures interrupted refueling for two hours, and the launch time moved from 9:38 to 10:38 Tuesday morning. The delay allowed the astronauts an extra hour of sleep, but they rose early anyway, too excited to remain in bed.

At breakfast, they found an arrangement of roses and American flags gracing their table, as well as a cake decorated with their mission emblem. In high spirits, Judy Resnik had a second serving of steak. Ellison Onizuka grumbled about the cold weather, but his smile belied his grumpiness.

After dressing in their blue jumpsuits, the astronauts made their way to the conference room where a final briefing awaited them. Reporters fired questions at them and the crew smiled, waved, and answered good-naturedly.

"It's a beautiful day for a launch," Dick Scobee called to the reporters.

"Then you're ready to fly?"

"Always," Scobee said. "I can't believe that I get paid to do what I love so much."

In the briefing, officials informed the astronauts of icy conditions on the pad and warned of a possible delay in launch time. No one mentioned last night's heated discussion about the reliability of the O-rings.

A modified Airstream trailer dubbed the Astrovan transported the crew to the launch pad elevator that carried them to the catwalk 150 feet above ground. From the outdoor walkway they entered the white room, a staging compartment pressed to the side of the shuttle somewhat like the mobile corridor that allows egress from a commercial airplane. In the white room, the fliers finished dressing for the flight, donning helmets and flight vests. As Christa McAuliffe dressed, the technician who had worn a mortarboard the day before greeted her with a bright red apple.

NASA had adopted the familiar teacher's symbol as part of the mission patch design, along with a depiction of Halley's Comet.

"Thanks," McAuliffe said. "Save it for me and I'll eat it when I get back."

Another technician produced a crew photo and asked for autographs.

"My son will hang it in his classroom," he said.

Each crewmember signed the photo. Following her usual custom, McAuliffe personalized her signature by adding "Reach For The Stars!"

Before the fliers climbed into the shuttle, the ground crew wiped the soles of each astronaut to keep dirt and contamination from entering the craft. Ron was the last crewmember in and sat next to the hatch.

As they settled into their seats, Scobee asked, "Ron, would you eyeball that hatch lock?"

My brother examined the formerly uncooperative lock and reported, "Everything looks good."

A NASA flight official studied the icicles hanging on the launch structure. Some were two feet long. He worried that dislodged icicles could strike the shuttle during lift-off and cause damage to the thermal protection system.

"We're going to stop the clock for a while," he told the astronauts, "and give that ice more time to melt."

"Commander understands a T equals zero no earlier than 11:08," Scobee said, relaying the information to the rest of the crew. "Everybody hear that?"

"Unfortunately," Greg Jarvis moaned.

"So, not so fast," Scobee agreed.

Recalling the five hours spent strapped into the cockpit seats the day before, Smith said, "I feel like I'm at the four-hour point of yesterday."

Resnik commiserated. "I feel like I'm past it," she said. "My butt is numb already."

"Maybe we could massage that for you," Jarvis offered, and the cockpit filled with laughter.

After another ice inspection and an update of the navigational computers to compensate for the delays, the countdown resumed at 11:29 A.M. at T-minus 9 minutes.

Inside the shuttle, the astronauts worked through the pre-flight checklist. The crew compartment contained two levels. On the upper deck Commander Dick Scobee sat before the control and instrument panels with pilot Michael Smith strapped into the seat to his right. Between them and immediately behind sat Judy Resnik. Ellison Onizuka was to her right. On the lower mid-deck were Ron in the rear and on the left, then Christa McAuliffe, and on the far right Greg Jarvis. The four astronauts on the upper deck had responsibilities during the launch and flight, but the three on the mid-deck could sit back and savor the ride. Ron was likely to enjoy it more than his seatmates. On the mid-deck, only he had access to a window. Perhaps he was pondering his duties in launching a satellite later that day or anticipating the orbital saxophone performance NASA had approved at the eleventh hour.

In high spirits, the crewmembers continued to crack jokes as the minutes crawled by.

"We could have ice skating on the launch platform," Scobee quipped.

Still complaining about the chill, Onizuka muttered, "Kind of cold this morning."

Smith decided to needle the warm-blooded Hawaiian. The pilot's seat allowed him to feel the sunshine entering the window, but Onizuka sat back in the shadow of the cabin.

"Up here, Ellison, the sun's shining in," Smith remarked. "My nose is freezing," Onizuka grumbled

"They're probably making a fortune selling coffee and doughnuts out at the viewing areas," Jarvis said.

"We should have gotten some," Scobee commented.

In the spectator grandstands the mood was festive. Hawkers sold buttons and memorabilia, especially merchandise showcasing Christa McAuliffe. A group of third-graders had a banner inscribed, "Go Christa!" In New Hampshire, the proud students of Concord High School prepared to cheer their beloved Mrs. McAuliffe into space. Yesterday had been a letdown, but the students waited to break out party hats and noisemakers for today's launch.

As the catwalk pulled away from the ship and umbilicals disengaged, Scobee said, "Seven minutes."

"Bye-bye," Resnik added. "Tighten your straps."

Launch control reminded the crew to lower their visors as the countdown proceeded.

"Roger," Scobee acknowledged. To the crew he said, "Welcome to space, guys. Two minutes downstairs."

"Okay, there goes the lox arm," Smith said, referring to the liquid oxygen feed that topped off the fuel tanks.

"Doesn't it go the other way?" Onizuka joked in mock panic.

Over the crew's laughter, Smith said, "God, I hope not, Ellison."

"One minute downstairs," Scobee announced. Then, "Thirty seconds…"

At T minus 30 seconds, the on-board flight computers took over the countdown and automated functions continued to prepare the *Challenger* for flight. The booster nozzles rotated to insure their readiness to steer the ship. From a nearby water tower, thousands of gallons of water erupted onto the launch pad to muffle the impending explosive burst of acoustic energy when the engines fired. The fail-safe self-destruct mechanism was armed in each solid-rocket booster, in case of a runaway shuttle, NASA could explode the rocket boosters to prevent the shuttle from crashing into a populated area.

At T minus 10 seconds *Challenger's* computers authorized engine ignition. Heat elements blazed beneath the three main engines to burn away excess hydrogen that may have collected there. Main engine three thundered to life, vomiting flame and smoke. Milliseconds later the other two engines followed suit.

"There they go, guys," Scobee said, exhilaration apparent in his voice.

"All right!" Resnik cried.

The engines throttled to 100% power. On-board computers confirmed proper functioning. Towering billows of steam rose from beneath the shuttle as engine flame vaporized the water released from the tower.

Hugh Harris, launch commentator and the public voice of NASA, finished the countdown: "…four, three, two, one, and lift-off."

On computer command the massive bolts at the base of each solid-rocket booster exploded and the Challenger began to rise.

"All riiiight!" Resnik yelled again.

"Here we go," Smith said.

Ron must have watched through the window as the shuttle lifted and the launch tower fell away. In seven seconds the spacecraft cleared the tower and was already moving at nearly 150 miles per hour.

"Lift-off of the twenty-fifth space shuttle mission," Harris announced, "and it has cleared the tower."

Once clear of the launch tower, the computers swiveled the rocket nozzles to fire in opposite directions, rotating the Challenger so that as the shuttle climbed, the crew would be upside down in relation to the ground. The flipping of the shuttle diminished aerodynamic stress during the ascent.

Smith, exhilarated by his first launch, caught the excitement Ron had so often described to me. "Go, you mother," he yelled.

Scobee radioed Houston that the Challenger had initiated the roll program.

At Mission Control in Houston, astronaut Richard Covey served as capcom, the on-ground communicator with the space-bound crew.

"Roger roll, Challenger," Covey confirmed.

Thirty-five seconds into the flight, Scobee announced, "Point nine," indicating that the shuttle's speed was nine-tenths the speed of sound. One second later, the *Challenger's* engines throttled down to sixty-five percent in order to ease the shuttle through so-called Max Q, the period of maximum aerodynamic stress.

The crew felt the ship waver slightly due to air turbulence, and Smith commented, "Looks like we've got a lot of wind here today."

"Yeah," Scobee agreed.

"There's Mach 1," Smith informed the crew.

"Okay, we're throttling down," Scobee said.

At forty-five seconds into the flight, all systems looked solid. The engines ran at sixty-five percent, and the instrument panel indicated that all systems were functioning properly. The *Challenger* traveled at a speed slightly above 1,500 miles per hour at a height of four nautical miles and a down-range distance of three miles.

A few seconds later, on-board computers began to raise the rocket engines toward the desired 104 % thrust.

"Throttling up," Scobee said.

At fifty-eight seconds into the mission, distant tracking cameras registered the first indication of trouble. A plume of smoke, invisible to the crew, trailed from the right-hand solid-rocket booster. A flicker of fire appeared on the same booster. Within milliseconds came a continuous gout of flame.

Oblivious to the approaching disaster, Smith again voiced his thrill.

"Feel that mother go!"

The flame grew in size and intensity as the fire licked at the external fuel tank.

"Thirty-five thousand, going through one point five," Smith said, informing the crewmembers on the mid-deck of altitude and speed.

The plume of smoke abruptly enlarged and changed shape. The fire erupting from the failed O-ring had breached the liquid fuel tank and seeping hydrogen fed the fire. A glow appeared on the external fuel tank at the site of the flame.

On-board instruments registered a massive pressure drop in the liquid hydrogen tank, but apparently events moved so rapidly that no one noted the aberrant readings. Even if Scobee or Smith had recognized the problem, they were powerless to extinguish the fire. The events of the next seven seconds played out with heart-breaking inevitability.

At Mission Control in Houston, capcom Covey relayed the order to push the engines to full power.

"*Challenger*, go with throttle up."

"Roger," Scobee replied, his voice betraying no awareness of the angry flames wrapping around the fuel tank. "Go with throttle up."

Three seconds later Mission Control received the final voice transmission from the *Challenger*. The last words belonged to pilot Michael Smith. Perhaps responding to instrument indications of engine trouble or falling pressure in the fuel tank, Smith said, "Uh-oh..."

The inarticulate words were infinitely expressive. Those two mumbled syllables communicated surprise, fear, disappointment, regret, and resignation, a radio-wave epitaph for a grand human endeavor gone tragically awry.

The crew compartment was jolted to the right, then back to the left. The fuselage twisted violently to the left, slapping the astronauts with twelve G's of sudden acceleration. A ball of hellish flame enveloped the shuttle.

A heartbeat later the vessel exploded in a cataclysm of blazing engine fuel.

Traveling at roughly twice the speed of sound, the *Challenger* broke into large pieces. The nose section containing the crew compartment tore away cleanly from the rest of the ship. The nose continued rising, dangling wires, tubes, and umbilicals in its wake like a parody of a kite's tail. Electrical power, instrumentation, and radio contact fled with the detached fuselage.

A ground crew spokesman, not yet aware of the conflagration overhead, briefly continued his running commentary as if all were well.

"One minute fifteen seconds. Velocity 2,900 feet per second. Altitude nine nautical miles. Downrange distance seven nautical miles…"

Sensing the stunned silence in the control room, he lifted his eyes to the television monitor. His words trailed off in mid-sentence.

With the nose ripped free, the payload bay section gaped open and the influx of air burst the compartment like an over-inflated balloon, spilling the communication satellite and the Halley's comet observation platform into the frigid air. The shuttle wings spun away. Debris rained toward the Atlantic Ocean 46,000 feet below.

One solid-rocket booster catapulted from the fiery cloud, its parachute vainly deploying as it fell. The other booster emerged from the smoke still rocketing skyward. Lacking computer control, the escaped rockets might veer inland toward populated areas. A command from the safety officer at Cape Canaveral Air Force Base activated the self-destruct munitions built into the rockets and they exploded in mid-air.

Inside the crew compartment, the astronauts were still conscious, at least for a few moments. Each crewman carried a PEAP, a personal egress air pack, to use if cabin pressure and air supply failed. At least three of the PEAPs later recovered by salvage divers had been manually activated.

A few seconds later, a NASA spokesman reported the brutally obvious.

"Flight controllers here are looking very carefully at the situation," he said. "Obviously a major malfunction. We have no downlink."

On the ground, spectators in the grandstands stared into the sky in numb confusion at first. The cheers and whoops of joy that began at ignition gave way to bewildered disbelief.

"Should there be so much smoke?"

"Did you see fire?"

"I think something's gone wrong."

The uncertainty quickly turned into sobs, as weeping onlookers clutched each other for comfort. In horror they watched the grim spectacle overhead, hating the vision before them but unable to look away. The spectators and well-wishers included Ellison Onizuka's wife Lorna, his brother Claude, and sixty-five friends and relatives; Steve McAuliffe and his two small children, nine-year-old Scott and six-year-old Caroline, who asked their dad what was happening; Judy Resnik's proud father; Greg Jarvis' parents from nearby Orlando; Mike Smith's family, his old friend and flight teacher Bob Burrows; Cheryl and the children, her parents, Harold and Verdell Moore, Mom and other family members.

They wrestled with shock and emotions too bitter for the heart to immediately accept, as the expanding white and gray cloud stretched contrail tentacles into the heavens. I can imagine the thoughts racing through the minds of frightened spectators. Maybe it isn't as bad as it seems. NASA must have things under control, a back-up plan, an emergency rescue option. They'll be all right. They have to be. This can't be happening. Maybe I'm still in bed, and I'll wake up soon. Dear God, don't let this be. Please, please…

The public announcer, voice breaking, said, "We have the report from the flight dynamics officer that the vehicle has exploded."

The shuttle nose containing the crew continued to rise for another twenty-five seconds, propelled by momentum and the concussive force of the explosion. From a height of 48,000 feet the crew cabin mounted to 65,000 feet before gravity overcame their climb for the stars. The twelve-mile drop lasted slightly more than two minutes. From the moment of breakup to the 200 miles-per-hour impact with the ocean, two minutes and forty-five seconds elapsed. No one knows how many crewmembers, if any, remained conscious through that long fall.

Immediate family members viewed the launch from a privileged position on the rooftop of a Space Center building. NASA personnel brought them indoors to share as much information as they had available. Lorna Onizuka slumped against a wall and slid to the floor. A few minutes later, Bruce Jarvis succumbed to shock and a doctor was summoned. Christa McAuliffe's children wept. Between sobs of grief, they questioned why they were told, 'nothing would go wrong.' In a nearby viewing room, a sixty-nine-year-old solid rocket engineer slumped over his desk, stricken by a heart attack. A life squad rushed him to the hospital where he later died.

Although ocean rescue teams were scrambling, aerospace officials knew that the astronauts were certainly dead. Mission Control at both Houston and Kennedy ordered a lockdown at both facilities, moving immediately to gather and protect every byte of available data and every millimeter of film footage. They could do nothing for the crew; they could only try to find out what went wrong in order to safeguard future flights.

At Morton Thiokol, the manufacturer of the solid-rocket boosters, white-faced engineers roamed from room to room, weeping openly. Those who opposed the flight berated themselves for not pressing their concerns more forcefully. If they had, maybe launch officials would have listened. Maybe those seven brave people would still be alive.

In the Concord High School auditorium, students cried and moaned. Teachers hugged one another in shared grief for their fallen colleague. The party hats suddenly felt as heavy as lead and the paper horns left the taste of ashes on the lips of students who had cheered jubilantly only moments before. The principal emptied the auditorium and sent the students home. He cancelled classes for the next day and made arrangements for counseling services for the stricken youngsters.

Along with cable stations, the three major television networks broke into programming to announce the disaster. The film of the explosion and the expanding cloud of smoke played endlessly. At least one news anchor publicly apologized for the ongoing reruns, but they continued to air, branding the national memory with a scene of unspeakable grief.

Along the coastal highway in Florida, motorists pulled to the side of the road, exited their cars, and stared into the eastern sky. The bells of nearby St. Paul Baptist Church tolled a mournful dirge, a memorial for the fallen heroes.

———

CHAPTER 17

Overcoming Tragedy

After rising early and waiting in vain for the launch on Monday, we made the tiring drive back to Atlanta. We arrived late, dragging from fatigue and emotional letdown. When we arrived at our house, Eric left us and drove to his home; Dad stayed with Mary and me. We slept late the next morning, but I rose early enough to watch the launch on television. I decided to let Dad and Mary sleep. I knew that they needed the rest, and they could catch the high points of the launch in news summaries later. Besides, we had an insider on the flight who would give us a blow-by-blow account in a few days.

I was a few minutes late for the lift-off. I turned the television on, went to the kitchen for a glass of orange juice; when I returned the screen showed the explosion and the expanding cloud of smoke.

On the television screen, the face of a broadcaster replaced the film of the explosion. I couldn't understand what he said. My mind was so filled with horror that I couldn't make sense of his words.

They showed the explosion again. I stood in the middle of the room, rooted in front of the television. After they showed the explosion for the third time, the reporter's words sank in.

"...some trouble with the shuttle.... No details yet... apparently exploded before reaching orbit.... No word on the crew..."

Ron was dead. They were all dead. I knew that with unshakable conviction. No one had lived through that fireball. I watched the pieces tumble from the sky. I felt as if I was watching pieces of my life fall to earth. My brother was gone.

Tears cascaded down my cheeks as I woke Dad. He sat upright with a start and looked hard at me. I couldn't explain.

"They had a— You've got to see this," I said.

When he continued to stare at me, I said, "Dad, come look at the TV."

I couldn't think of anything else to say. Dad climbed from the bed, his movements sluggish from weariness or, perhaps, dread. In the living room the tape was playing again. Dad watched silently, fell into the nearest chair, and buried his face in his hands. In my whole life, I'd never seen my father cry.

How could I break this to Mary? She was pregnant. The shock...

My thoughts flitted to Ron's children.

And Cheryl.

How could God let this happen?

In the bedroom, Mary woke up to answer the phone beside

our bed. I didn't even hear it ring. The sound of my father's sobs drowned out every other sound in the world.

A friend phoned, saying to my wife, "Mary, I am so sorry."

Still sleepy, Mary replied, "What? What are you talking about?"

"You don't know?" the friend said. "You haven't— Mary, I'll call you back."

Mary came out of the bedroom to find both Dad and me weeping. I pointed to the television and choked out, "The shuttle exploded."

I needn't have worried about my wife. Her strength saw me through that sorrowful day. She came to me and held me in her arms for a long time.

I didn't know what to do next. I felt wrapped in cotton, my thoughts barely moving. Dad was equally lost, but Mary said, "Your mom is alone down there."

"Mom," I said. "We need to get back to Florida, get to Mom."

"You and your dad get dressed," she said. "I'll call the airlines."

"Yeah, we need to get a flight," I said, still a dozen mental steps behind her.

She dialed the phone, looked at me, and said, "Get dressed, Carl."

I continued to move as if I were wading through molasses. Mary made arrangements with Delta for emergency booking on an upcoming flight. While Dad and I stumbled around like zombies, my wife got us all packed and out the front door.

So many of my memories of those hours are disjointed and fragmentary. I remember coveys of reporters, but I don't know if they accosted us at our home, at the airport, or in both places. I don't think I responded to their questions in any way. Eric joined us at some point, maybe at the flight lounge. Again, I don't remember, just as the drive to the airport is an empty space in my memory. I made my feet move, carried the luggage Mary put in my hands, and tried to untangle the knot in my guts.

Our flight took us to Melbourne, Florida, about thirty miles from the Space Center. On the way we almost died in a plane crash. As our commercial plane descended toward the runway, a student pilot steered his small plane in an intersecting path with ours. The student panicked, ignored the control tower, and our pilot jarringly yanked us upward to avoid a mid-air collision. I almost laughed at the irony. My family was jetting to Florida where my brother had just died in a shuttle explosion and our plane almost crashed. At the thought of Ron, my eyes welled up and I felt wetness running down my face.

At Kennedy Space Center, many of the friends and supporters of the crewmembers had left for home. Why stay any longer? They could do nothing for the crew. They couldn't even reach relatives of the crew to give comfort. NASA had sequestered immediate family members, putting each family in a room at the astronauts' quarters.

I found my mother with her sister Mary, sitting silently in a room NASA had given them. I knelt beside the chair and hugged them.

"How are you holding up?" I asked.

Mom's only answer was a shrug.

"What happened?" she asked.

"There was a problem with the shuttle," I told her.

She nodded vacantly and looked away. I tried to engage her in conversation, but my mother went to a private place in her head when she wanted to avoid reality. She was there now, and only her outward presence sat in the room. I wondered if she comprehended the day's events. I knew she saw the *Challenger* lift off from the pad. Maybe her mind wouldn't let her see the explosion. Or, having seen the fiery ball raining debris, perhaps she refused to acknowledge the reality. As long as she denied Ron's death, she could hold that horror at bay.

She focused on me, as if just noticing my arrival.

"Did something happen?" she asked.

"The shuttle, Mom. There's a serious problem. Do you understand?"

She nodded again and returned to her private sanctuary.

I worried about her but didn't know how to help. She was as beyond my reach as Ron.

Vice-President George H. Bush and Senators Jake Garn and John Glenn flew from Washington to give official condolences to the families. NASA gathered us in a large room for their visit. We found Cheryl there. We all hugged and the tears started again.

"I'm sorry," I said. "He loved you so much."

"What am I going to do?" she asked.

"It will be all right," I said. "We'll get though this."

The assurances felt flat and empty, but I had to say something.

Before the dignitaries spoke, June Scobee asked if she could say a few words on behalf of the assembled families.

"We've been talking, and we all agree that this tragedy shouldn't mean the end of the space program," she said to the politicians. "My husband—"

She broke off, took a deep breath, and tried again.

"My husband believed in the exploration of space. He got into the program to help that happen. From talking to the other families this afternoon, I know that was true of everyone on the shuttle."

Around the room heads nodded and voices murmured in assent.

"If we let this...setback...halt the program, then those seven people died for no purpose. That's not what Dick would have wanted. None of them would have wanted that. Make their deaths count for something."

I knew she was right. In my heart, no advancement of knowledge or conquest of space could provide adequate compensation for my brother's death. Nevertheless, Ron would want the shuttle program to continue. He'd hate the notion that his death undermined an effort he supported so whole-heartedly in life. He would want his sacrifice to steel our national resolve. He would expect others to pick up the torch and carry the flame.

Each member of the Washington contingent spoke briefly to the group about sacrifice, courage, and perseverance. I deeply appreciated the gesture, but I didn't receive comfort from their words. Nothing would bring my brother back to me. This was too much to pay for science and technology. When John Glenn choked up briefly during his remarks, I suspected he was remembering his own career in space and picturing his loved ones in a situation like this.

After the impromptu speeches, the vice-president and senators mingled with the families, sharing hugs and tears. On another day, I'd have been more excited to shake hands with world-movers like these men. That day, everything felt flat. I spoke words, shook hands, moved around meeting other family members, but my emotions were detached from the scene.

President Ronald Reagan canceled the State of the Union address scheduled for that evening. Instead, he spoke to America from the oval office in the afternoon, giving voice to our national grief.

"We mourn seven heroes," he said. "We mourn their loss as a nation together."

A nation in grief. Even people who'd never met Ron, never heard him play the sax, felt the pang of his life snuffed out so suddenly. The thought eased my own grief, if only a little.

"For the families of the seven, we cannot bear, as you do, the full impact of this tragedy," the president said, gazing earnestly into the camera. "But we feel the loss. Your loved ones were daring and brave, and they had that special grace, that special spirit that says, 'Give me a challenge and I'll meet it with joy.' They had a hunger to explore the universe and discover its truths."

He might have been speaking directly to me about my brother. Those words described Ron so aptly.

"The future doesn't belong to the fainthearted," President Reagan said. "It belongs to the brave. The *Challenger* crew was pulling us into the future, and we'll continue to follow them."

I don't care about the future, I thought. I want the past back, the days when Ron lived and laughed.

President Reagan concluded his short memorial with a promise that America would remember the crew of the *Challenger* forever.

"The crew of the space shuttle *Challenger* honored us by the manner in which they lived their lives. We will never forget them, nor the last time we saw them this morning, — as they prepared for the journey and waved goodbye — and 'slipped the surly bonds of earth,' to 'touch the face of God.'"

Other members of our family drove from Lake City to join us in Florida. Like many African-Americans, we have a strong sense of family, and in times of trouble even members of the extended family gather for comfort and support. We appreciated the arrival of aunts, uncles, and cousins, but wanted to leave the Space Center. I didn't expect our lives to return to normalcy immediately; however, I wanted the reassurance of familiar surroundings and routines.

In a gesture both kind and genuinely helpful, South Carolina Lieutenant Governor Mike Daniel sent a plane for my family.

We flew first to Lake City to drop off my mother, then Dad, Mary, Eric, and I continued to Atlanta. When we arrived at home, reporters were encamped before our house. They threw questions at us and clamored for interviews.

"How do you feel about the tragedy?"

"Was NASA negligent in the launch?"

"Do you think the space program should continue?"

"We can't talk about th—"

I tried to explain, with microphones thrust into my face.

"Please let us throu—"

Again, rapid-fire questions cut me off.

We bulldozed through the reporters to find refuge in our home, but once inside I wandered the rooms as if I were a stranger. Fatigue dogged me, yet I couldn't sleep. When I tried talking to Mary, I merely mouthed platitudes and denials: "I can't believe he's gone," or "I talked to him just yesterday."

The phone rang often with friends calling to offer their sympathy or reporters asking for comments. I let Mary handle most of the calls, but each time I heard the ring a tiny flame of irrational hope blazed briefly and brilliantly in my heart. Maybe Ron was calling to say there was a crazy mix-up, and he wasn't on the shuttle when it lifted off.

In my imagination I rewrote history. If even a single delay on the launch hadn't happened, the *Challenger* would have flown in warmer weather with functional O-rings. If the car wreck injuries hadn't put Ron out of commission for months, he'd have been in a different rotation on the shuttle schedule, and flight 51-L would have lifted off without him. If Ron had contracted a stomach virus on Monday... I wove dozens of what-if possibilities, like the science fiction story in which the alteration of one detail in the past radically transforms the future.

For months after the accident, I nursed a secret fantasy that Ron and the others had escaped the shuttle before impact. They were on a deserted island safe, healthy, and eager for rescue. Sooner or later a fishing boat or a plane would discover them and my brother would return to a celebration dwarfing his last homecoming. I played that impossible scenario over and over in my mind. Intellectually, I knew Ron was never coming back, but the heart finds ways to ease its pain.

Three days after the disaster, NASA sponsored a memorial service for the *Challenger* crew. We flew to Houston to be with Cheryl and the bereaved relatives of the other crewmembers. The outdoor service included an address from President Reagan and other dignitaries. I wish I could report that the service comforted me and the words of tribute lifted my spirits. In fact, I remember almost nothing from the speeches and eulogies.

Only one aspect of the service remains bright and vivid in my memory. At the conclusion of the memorial, Air Force jets thundered through the clear sky in the "missing man formation". Flying in a V arrangement, the jets roared from the horizon. The thunder of engines mounted with their approach. When the planes were directly overhead, one jet pulled out of the chevron formation and mounted heavenward in a steep ascent.

I had sat numbly through the service, but the flying tribute struck me as unbearably poignant. A stabbing sense of loss overwhelmed me as one lonely jet soared away from its comrades. The broken V disappeared in the distance. I stared into the sky, watching the contrails dissipate slowly in the heights, remembering the expanding tendrils snaking from the cloud of smoke left behind by the *Challenger*. I inhaled deeply, a breath that nearly became a sob. I brought my eyes back to earth where spouses and parents embraced, exchanging comfort. I saw President Reagan shake hands with my father and offer condolences to Mom and Cheryl.

I looked to the heavens again, but the sky was utterly empty, a blue mirror of my empty soul.

"What now?" I asked softly. "Where do we go from here?"

I don't know if I spoke to myself, to Ron, or to the washed-out sky, but nobody answered.

CHAPTER 18

Ron's Mission Continues

The service at Houston was the first of many memorials for Ron and the *Challenger* crew. Within a few days we gathered again with our family for a service of remembrance at Wesley United Methodist Church in Lake City. Life-long friends and neighbors surrounded us as we sat in our childhood church, so rich with memories both happy and bittersweet.

While I appreciated the service in Houston, this one meant far more to me. This congregation consisted of hometown folks, people who knew Ron well. Many of them had played football at his side, shared campfire cooking on scouting trips, or picked bits of sodium from hair and clothing after my brother's unauthorized chemistry experiment. The conversations and stories reached beyond Ron's astronaut days and embraced his whole, rich life. The gathering in Houston had been entirely sad, but in Lake City we both laughed and cried at the sharing of favorite memories.

The church overflowed with folks from all walks of life who joined us to pay their last respects. Projection screens in the fellowship hall broadcasted the proceedings for guests who couldn't find room in the sanctuary. Along with the citizens of Lake City, dignitaries also joined us to share their condolences. Governor Dick Riley, Senators Strom Thurmond and Fritz Hollings, and the Rev. Jesse Jackson came to express their respect for my brother and to mourn his loss.

Our pastor, Rev. George McClenan, led the service. He celebrated Ron's life thoughtfully and gratefully. He was not our childhood pastor, but he met my brother on many occasions. He spoke as a friend of the family, not a stranger. He also testified to the resurrection and our certain hope of a life in Christ beyond this world. I was thankful today to sit in the church of my upbringing and hear the old and cherished promises of heaven once again.

I was expected to "say a few words" during the service. I rose and recalled aloud Ron's devotion to his friends, his family, and his God. My emotions ran high. I couldn't finish my short eulogy without breaking down. Although I choked up, I held back the tears until the choir sang, "If I can help somebody, then my living was not in vain…"

That beautiful song led me to reflect on Ron's life and how richly he blessed the world. I wondered sadly how much more he might have accomplished if the accident had not prematurely cut off his years. What strides might he have made in science? What breakthroughs would have emerged from his research? How many young men and women would he have encouraged to pursue careers in science? I hated to think of his contributions coming to an end. I wanted to find a way my brother could continue making a mark in the world. His life was over, but why should his influence also come to an end?

On the day of the memorial service, I experienced my greatest moment of joy when I emerged from the church and found my Omega Psi Phi fraternity brothers waiting for me. I plunged into the group on the steps of the church, shaking hands, hugging, and slapping backs. We joked, swapped stories of happy times, and kidded one another about embarrassing college escapades.

I had pledged Omega Psi Phi the spring of my sophomore year at North Carolina A & T, and Ron had followed me into the fraternity the next fall. One fraternity brother after another expressed his sadness over Ron's death, but their words were unnecessary. Their presence communicated all I needed to know. I appreciated these true friends who had traveled many miles for no reason except to share their support. Death ends many things, but not even death is strong enough to quench friendship and love.

More memorial services followed in the ensuing weeks. My brother had moved in many circles, and I felt as if every group to which Ron belonged planned a service. I didn't begrudge any of the memorials. I was touched that Omega Psi Phi planned an event in memory of my brother. I appreciated the services at the various churches where Ron had worshipped and taught karate. I gave thanks for events honoring Ron at A & T and MIT. In spite of my gratitude at the outpouring of regard for Ron, each service left me more drained and emotionally emaciated.

Our culture typically expects the bereaved to curtail their grieving and move on after the funeral flowers have wilted. We faced the opposite problem in the aftermath of Ron's death. Our emotional wounds re-opened with each memorial.

Healing came slowly for us. Although the many tributes to Ron honored his memory and made us proud, each service forced us to live through the events of January 28 with renewed vividness.

In the beginning I tried to be gracious and accept every memorial invitation. After attending ten services, I stopped participating. Each service ripped off the scab from my grief and left me bleeding again.

One final memorial approached that I could not avoid. Indeed, I welcomed this one. In April, NASA recovered the bodies of the astronauts from the ocean. After appropriate postmortem study, the agency released the remains of the shuttle crewmembers to their respective families. Cheryl decided Ron should be buried in the soil where he grew up. My brother had traveled around the world and lived in various cities, but South Carolina was his home. He came from Lake City, and we agreed with Cheryl that he should return there in the end.

Although I was emotionally drained by the repeated eulogies offered for Ron, I hoped that the physical burial of my brother's remains would grant me closure to the nightmare of the past three months. When Ron's casket was lowered into the rich South Carolina soil, maybe I could shed the pall that hung over my existence.

On a bright day in May, mourners packed into Wesley United Methodist Church. This funeral was more formal and carefully orchestrated than the earlier memorial service. Once again, dignitaries such as Jesse Jackson and Cicely Tyson arrived to add their condolences to the televised proceedings.

To my surprise and great satisfaction, all of Ron's crewmates from his first *Challenger* mission came to pay their respects to their fallen comrade. Their demeanor both dignified and somber, Bruce McCandless, Hoot Gibson, Vance Brand, and Robert Stewart entered the church with as little fanfare as possible. They spoke courteously to reporters, but avoided the limelight. They understood that any one of them could have been on that disastrous flight. The astronauts came not to garner goodwill for NASA, but to express their grief for a man who had worked at their side and earned their admiration.

I had felt compelled to speak at the service, but this time I chose to be a bereaved brother instead of a family spokesman. I listened to the now familiar remarks about courage and the cost of progress, but my spirit remained hollow and uncomforted. I didn't doubt the sincerity of those who spoke, nor could I deny that pioneers don't always live to enjoy the fruits of their own sacrifice. My head understood these things, but my heart still longed to bring my brother back.

When the service ended, the mourners filed out. We loaded the casket into the hearse, and the funeral procession wound its way from the church to the cemetery. The smell of spring in the air and the colorful swatches of newly blooming flowers belied the reason for our gathering under the cloudless sky. Eric and I served as pallbearers, helping to carry the casket across the green lawn and settling it gently on the supports over the open grave.

"Ashes to ashes and dust to dust," the minister intoned, scattering a handful of dirt beside the casket. "We commit the body of our departed brother to this resting place in the sure and certain hope of the resurrection in Jesus Christ."

The first faint hum of distant jets stole through the air, mounting steadily to a roar as the planes came into sight and then rocketed overhead in the missing man formation. As the jets diminished in the distance, the commanding officer of the honor guard barked, "Present arms!" The military guards lifted rifles in unison, shouldered the stocks, and fired the twenty-one-gun salute in a unison burst of thunder.

Then it was over—the prayers finished, the jets returning to base, visitors making farewells, and the cemetery workers standing at a discreet distance, waiting for the crowd to disperse so they could finish their work and call it a day. I searched my feelings and discovered no relief, no tranquility, and no release. I felt numb and tired, profoundly weary, and vaguely guilt-ridden by my continuing grief. Now was the time to move on, to suck it in, and get on with life. I left the cemetery knowing that life had to go on and wondering how to do that.

If Ron's demise had been my only burden, I might have handled things better, but other deaths in the family added to the grinding weight on my shoulders. Grandmother had been very ill when the *Challenger* launched in January, much too sick to make the trip to Florida. That good woman died quietly five months after the shuttle explosion. Only a few weeks later, before I could come to terms with Grandmother's death, Granddaddy followed her to heaven. The following month Grandmother's sister also passed on. I was suddenly bereft of my life-long friend and brother, as well as the beloved role models who had supported and guided me from birth.

My life became a perpetual funeral. Death surrounded me on every side. My grief was a black hole sucking the joy and light from my days. Life felt like a mere interim before dying.

Although young and healthy, I couldn't shake the feeling that my own death was near. I went through the motions of living while waiting for the end.

In a sense, I was already dead—deceased and dried up on the inside. Ron was born only ten months after me. I couldn't remember a time without my brother. We grew up together, dressed alike, played the same games. School, church, sports, Scouts—we shared everything. For more than twenty-five years virtually every area of my life included Ron. Even after he moved away to California and later to Texas, we spoke often and visited whenever we could. The mid-air explosion of the shuttle killed not only my brother, but also a vital part of me. Growing up so near in age, Ron and I were like twins. His death was the loss of my other self.

I might have succumbed to the night growing inside me if not for the birth of my first and only child in July. With the help of this beautiful child given to me by Mary, I took my first steps out of the darkness. When I laid eyes on precious Desiree' I discovered anew that life deserves to be fully embraced. Holding my daughter's tiny form in my arms, gazing into her unfocused eyes, I realized that simply being in this world is a blessing. In spite of the hardships and disappointments, the sheer thrill of living is worth the effort. Cradling my daughter against my chest justified every moment of struggle I had endured to reach this day.

As tired and clichéd as it may sound, caressing Desiree's cheek with my rough fingers reassured me that life does indeed go on. The world that Ron once orbited in space was still spinning on its axis, still circling the life-giving sun, and every dawn was a priceless gift. When we open our eyes in the morning, God spreads endless possibilities before us. And when we lay ourselves down at the end of the day—or at the end of all our days—we look back over more blessings than we could ever name. I had begun to think that death renders life futile. In fact, the inevitability of death reminds us to redeem each day and to enrich our passage through this world with as much love and courage as we can muster. That's how Ron lived his life; he'd be disappointed if I did any less with mine.

With Desiree's birth, I began the long climb from the pit of my grief. Healing doesn't happen all at once. Even twenty years later, tears sometimes surprise me when I'm remembering some moment from Ron's life or relating his story. Although I still miss him, I've accepted my brother's death, and I've found sources of comfort that console me.

I continually give thanks that Ron's memory lives on, and his example inspires others to follow in his footsteps. In Lake City, the main street now bears Ron's name, as does the school we once attended. For kids in our hometown, he is both a local hero and a role model. His success in life encourages them to reach high and to believe in themselves. If little Ron McNair from the other side of the tracks could construct lasers and fly into outer space, then other Lake City boys and girls can go as far as they want.

Of course, my brother's influence reaches beyond his hometown. In his former neighborhood in Houston, children play in a park established in his memory. At Wheeler Baptist Church, where Ron served as "Minister of Defense", karate students hone their skills in the Ron McNair Activity Center. Students perform important aerospace research in the Ronald E. McNair Building at the Massachusetts Institute of Technology.

One struggling student confided in me that hearing Ron's story changed his life. Inspired by Ron's perseverance, the student dedicated his schoolwork to my brother's memory. He brought his C's up to A's, eventually earning a Ph.D. in physics like his role model. Today he works for a national company, advancing the kind of scientific contributions Ron might have made had he lived longer.

Admonishing students to work hard and envision a bright future often sounds like a pie-in-the-sky sermon, especially for disadvantaged youth. The setbacks and negative images fostered by our culture make it much easier to settle for failure than to believe in success. But Ron's story makes a powerful impact without preaching. Hearing about my brother's struggles puts a face on the dream of success. Ron loved mentoring youngsters and instilling in them a love for learning and the determination to press toward the highest goals. Although my brother isn't here to continue that work in person, his undefeatable spirit still elevates ambitions and transforms lives.

Apart from my brother's gift for improving the lives of others, I also find reassurance in knowing that Ron himself had a wonderful, exuberant life filled with passion and happiness. My brother loved everything he did. When life threw him a curve ball, he stepped up to the plate and swung mightily.

For instance, NASA surprised him with the photography assignment on his first shuttle flight. Instead of whining about his inexperience or grumbling that someone else should take the job, Ron became instantly passionate about photos and videography. By the launch date, he could scarcely wait to get his hands on the camera and begin recording the flight.

Wearing his director's beret and opening each video scene with his director's clapper slate, he turned the photo assignment into a grand adventure. As a result, his photographic work is displayed in planetariums and science books around the world. In doing this, he added another prestigious award to his impressive list of accomplishments.

Ron had fun and he enjoyed life to the fullest. He zealously pursued anything that caught his interest. Although he died far too young at the age of thirty-five, Ron crammed his brief existence with more energy, excitement, and enjoyment than do most people who live twice as long.

We can't evaluate a person's life by the pages on a calendar. When a piece of music elevates my spirit and moves me to tears, I don't use a stopwatch to judge the worth of that song. I don't choose a movie based on its running time. When I consider my favorite books, the ones that have enriched and enlarged me, the page count is irrelevant to the quality of the writing.

Neither can we judge a life by its length. As is true of so many things, quality matters more than quantity. According to the poet, the candle that burns at both ends doesn't last long, but while burning it brightens the world with a beautiful light. Regardless of its brevity, Ron's life shone brilliantly.

My brother died experiencing his ultimate thrill. I remember him repeatedly watching the video of his first lift-off, volume at maximum, the floorboards vibrating with the roar of the rocket engines. He never had another experience as viscerally exciting as the launch. The shuttle launch represented a mountaintop moment, a rare personal peak. Ron died in the process of experiencing that incredible moment a second time;

I can imagine worse ways to leave this world.

Given absolutely certain knowledge of the *Challenger's* explosion, no sane person would have entered that craft. We mortals are rarely granted such certainty. Instead, we weigh the risks, balance the benefits, and make our best choice.

Ron certainly understood the risks inherent in strapping frail human flesh into a four million-pound projectile and riding an explosive inferno into space. His analytical mind considered the possibilities and decided that the trip warranted the risk. One more chance to mount the behemoth and leap into the sky, another opportunity to garner new learning, the possibility of improving life for others—in Ron's mind, these gains offset the possible cost. He decided to live boldly, reach for accomplishment, and face the risks. As much as I miss him, I know he was right to fly.

Ron's determination to get the most from life reminds me of a parable Jesus once told. A wealthy man summoned three servants and allocated various amounts of money for them to use on his behalf while he was out of town. When he returned after a lengthy absence, he called the servants for an accounting. The master was well pleased with two of the servants who had invested his money and earned a return. The third servant, afraid to risk the money entrusted to him, had buried the entire sum in the ground in order to keep it safe. The disappointed and angry master took the money from the fearful servant and gave it to the first servant. God does not mean us to hoard our gifts or hide from life. The faithful servant puts himself on the line and faces the risks while entrusting the outcome to God.

Ron had an explorer's spirit, the courage that offers great gifts in a great cause. Some men are not meant for the humdrum life of the daily round. In an earlier era, my brother would have sailed for Africa, trudged across the ice in search of the South Pole, or ridden the winds in a hot-air balloon. Instead, he pressed the frontiers of knowledge and sailed into space.

By strange coincidence, he died exactly 390 years to the day after the death of Sir Francis Drake, the great explorer. The oceans provided the frontiers in the sixteenth century, and few seafarers pushed farther than Drake. The English navigator endured storms, warfare, and disease on his voyages, but his restless heart belonged to the sea. He became the first Englishman to circumnavigate the globe.

Drake's many accomplishments earned him a knighthood and a seat in Parliament. Most men would have settled into the good life and basked in the afterglow of youthful adventures, but not Drake. At the age of forty-five he took ship again and spent another decade on the high seas. He died on board ship far from home in the Caribbean. The crew gave his body to the depths, entrusting their captain to the sea he loved so fervently.

Sir Francis Drake died doing what he loved. No warm cocoa, easy chair, and comfortable retirement for the man who had sailed around the world. Death comes in many forms. For a true explorer, the death of a stifled spirit is worse than physical death. A single journey might encompass a lifetime of passionate adventure. Conversely, years of the uneventful daily routine may constitute a slow dying. What a waste for an intrepid seeker like Sir Francis Drake—or Ronald McNair— to spend his days in a safe harbor when his spirit longed for the open sea.

When asked to describe the experience of flying in space

and looking down at the distant earth, Ron replied in the spirit of the true explorer.

"You really cannot tell anybody that," he said. "Words, pictures, films—nothing is like being there."

Ron's groping effort to express the inexpressible calls to my mind the words of the apostle Paul when he vainly attempted to describe heaven to the Corinthian Christians. "No eye has seen, no ear has heard, no mind has conceived what God has prepared for those who love him."

As for heaven, I guess nothing is like being there. We earthbound creatures of flesh and blood can't possibly picture the glory of living with God. We talk about streets of gold and heavenly mansions, but whatever Christ has prepared for his people is beyond anything our little minds can imagine. What a place to explore! As usual, Ron the pioneer got there ahead of me.

I read about the explorer Vasco de Gama in a long-ago history class. In de Gama's day sailors called the southern tip of Africa the Cape of Storms. Violent weather haunted that expanse of sea. No ship had yet survived the attempt to sail around the cape. Cartographers marked that spot with dire warnings; wise sailors feared and shunned the Cape of Storms.

But Vasco de Gama dared to venture where no one else would sail. Risking everything, he steered into those treacherous seas and safely rounded the African cape. Beyond the crashing waves and the raging storms, the Portuguese explorer discovered a vast, calm sea and safe passage to the immense wealth of India. After that, the map makers changed the name of that point from the Cape of Storms to the Cape of Good Hope.

Some believe that death is the final storm that shipwrecks all our hopes and sinks every dream, but I am not one of those people. Although I can't see beyond the Cape of Storms, I believe a peaceful sea awaits us on the other side. The Bible calls Jesus Christ the pioneer of our faith because he sailed through the storm of death and came back to tell us, "Don't be afraid. There's a good place, a safe place, waiting for you on the other side." Christ turns death into a new beginning. For those who entrust their lives into his care, Christ turns the Cape of Storms into the Cape of Good Hope. Christians live by hope—the hope of a risen Lord who never fails his people.

Whatever else might be said about my brother, at the top of the list write these words: "He was a Christian." I never knew Ron to falter in his faith. His trust in Jesus Christ was the central truth of his life. Everything else flowed from that crucial commitment. That basic certainty informed his every decision and shaped his every action.

I cherish Ron's comment on his first *Challenger* mission when he told Grandmother, "I wouldn't have set foot inside that space shuttle if Jesus wasn't there first."

I treasure those words, and they comfort me when I think of that tragic explosion in the skies over Florida. What was true on Ron's first flight was equally certain on his second. History records seven crewmembers on Shuttle Mission 51-L. The cameras on January 28 recorded the entrance of seven passengers into the *Challenger*, but faith assures me of an additional rider, the unseen but undeniable presence of Jesus. In his last moments my brother faced death at the side of the One who has conquered the grave and promised eternal victory to all who place their trust in his love. Ron did not slip alone into the great unknown. Instead he left this world in the company of a faithful Guide who led him by the hand to a place prepared for his coming.

Two minutes and forty-five seconds elapsed from the time of the booster explosion to the impact in the sea. Two minutes and forty-five seconds is long enough to recite the Lord's Prayer or pray the words of Psalm 139: *"You hem me in-behind and before; you have laid your hand upon me.... Where can I go from your Spirit? Where can I flee from your presence? If I go up to the heavens, you are there; if I make my bed in the depths, you are there. If I rise on the wings of the dawn, if I settle on the far side of the sea, even there your hand will guide me, your right hand will hold me fast."*

Two minutes and forty-five seconds is time enough to give thanks for a life lived to the fullest and to ask God's blessing on those left behind.

In two minutes and forty-five seconds Ron had time to reach out to someone else in that crowded crew cabin and say, "Don't be afraid. This is not the end."

My brother was not one to waste time. Two minutes and forty-five seconds was time enough to praise God, to confront death with courage, and to prepare for the next frontier.

In the days after Ron's departure, people repeatedly asked me, "How are you doing? How is your mom doing? Your dad? How are Cheryl and the children?"

I found myself often replying, "I don't know. I'm not sure."

In retrospect, I realize no one asked me the one question I could have answered with absolute certainty. I wish someone had asked me, *"How is Ron doing?"*

I would have said then what I still say today.

Ron is okay.

My little brother is doing just fine.

Epilogue

On March 15, 2004, the citizens of Lake City, South Carolina dedicated the Dr. Ronald E. McNair Memorial Park. Ironically, we had to schedule the dedication twice. On the original date of January 28—the eighteenth anniversary of the *Challenger* tragedy—an ice storm shut down my hometown, reminiscent of the freakish freezing temperatures that led to the shuttle explosion. After emergency crews restored power to cold, dark homes and cleared away the devastation of broken limbs and trees uprooted by the weight of freezing rain, we gathered again in March for a more successful dedication.

Ron's widow, Cheryl, and their children, Reggie and Joy, joined my brother Eric and me along with our families at the Lake City Presbyterian Church for a pre-dedication service. The passing years had dulled the edge of grief, and we gratefully remembered the ways in which Ron blessed us and gave thanks for his life among us.

From the church we proceeded to the newly raised monument on Main Street in the heart of downtown Lake

City and mounted to our place on the podium. A smile spread across my face as I surveyed the bronzed statue of Ron. The artist had skillfully captured my brother in metal—not just his outward appearance, but his spirit as well. Posed in his NASA flight suit with helmet under one arm, Ron's body language communicated confidence and courage.

A marble wall stretches forty feet beside the memorial inscribed with quotes from Ron. The centerpiece of the monument is the mastaba containing Ron's remains, exhumed a few weeks earlier from their resting place in Lake City's Rest Lawn Memorial Park. A shimmering pool surrounds the mastaba, bestowing the memorial with tranquil beauty. My brother would probably argue that the central focus is not his entombed remains, but the eternal flame that burns day and night before the mastaba. That would be just like Ron to emphasize life over death and God's goodness over human accomplishments.

As we stood on the platform listening to choirs sing about faith and bravery, I thanked God that not only was Ron's memory enshrined, but also his spirit was still alive and abroad.

After Ron's funeral in 1986, the McNair family retreated to Mom's living room, wondering how to honor the memory of a good and gifted man who had touched so many hearts.

"Whatever we do," Dad said, "we don't need to make Ron bigger in death than he was in life. He wouldn't want that."

"Ron would want a memorial that helped somebody," Eric said.

"That's right," I agreed. "If we're going to remember Ron,

let's do something good in his name."

As we wept and laughed together, remembering Ron's love for physics, we decided to create a scholarship fund to help disadvantaged youth study science and technology. Maybe we could make an easier path for the next science student from an impoverished background.

With research and reflection we refined that basic idea. We discovered that a number of similar scholarship programs already existed, so we looked for a different niche. Many youths, particularly minorities, don't realize the possibilities of a career in science or technology. They set their sights on more familiar jobs, assuming that scientific study and research are beyond their reach. If no one challenges this defeatist attitude, America will lose a whole generation of potential scientists and technical professionals drawn from the rich diversity of our national culture. Ron's life offers indisputable proof that a humble beginning is no insurmountable barrier for an intelligent and precocious mind. If we could encourage and challenge others to follow in Ron's footsteps, we might build a better future for everybody.

This was the inspiration behind the Dr. Ronald E. McNair Foundation, an ongoing effort to interest economically challenged youth in the study of science, mathematics, and technology.

Against the background of the high school band playing for the dedication of the Memorial, I heard Ron's voice in my head, declaring, "I believe that in our urban and rural cities there are great minds and talents with hands that can control a spacecraft with the same dexterity that they control and handle a basketball. These talents must not be wasted."

Ron would be the first to celebrate the foundation's mission to encourage a passion for science and mathematics among youngsters of different races, nationalities, and backgrounds.

The choir began another song as the March wind plucked at my coat. My brother's remains might be sealed in the mastaba, but his influence continues to touch multitudes. I thankfully considered the Ronald E. McNair Post-Baccalaureate Achievement Program (McNair Scholars Program), a federally-funded initiative that provides financial assistance and graduate school preparation for first-generation, economically disadvantaged or under-represented college students. What would my usually restrained brother say if he knew that over 20,000 college scholars have received assistance from a program bearing his name?

My gaze swept the crowd gathered for the dedication, and the thought of hometown love warmed me on that chilly day. The Memorial Park for my brother had cost nearly two million dollars. While some of the funding had come through grants from the mayor's office, most of the donations arrived in dribs and drabs from working class people from every walk of Lake City life. Teachers, farmers, small business owners, blacks and whites worked together to raise the money for this memorial. Of those who contributed, most eked out a living on less than a middle-class income. Some dipped into savings or retirement provisions to give to the memorial fund. Some actually took out second mortgages on their homes in order to support the monument. Today's celebration consummated fifteen years of effort and sacrifice. Some who gave to the project did not live to see it realized.

My eyes watered, and not entirely because of the persistent spring wind. I am as proud to claim these decent, God-fearing people, as they are to claim Ron.

Mary nudged my arm and I drew my attention back to the dedication ceremony. On cue, Cheryl knelt and solemnly kindled the eternal flame. As she stood and stepped back, a gust of wind battered the flame. The tongue of fire shrank, quivered before the blast, and then rose straight and proud. As the fire took hold, applause erupted from the crowd. Cheers and amens rose into the sky, soaring boldly and joyfully toward distant heavens and unseen stars.

Dr. Ronald E. McNair Foundation's Educational Collaborations and Partnerships

Ronald E. McNair Post-Baccalaureate Achievement Programs

(an undergraduate Ph.D. preparation program) at one hundred seventy-nine (179) universities and colleges nationally.

Institutions of higher learning that have provided facilities and sites for the McNair Space and Science Camp Program

Clark Atlanta University
DeVry University
Kennesaw State University
Life University
Morris Brown College

Clayton State College
Georgia Institute of Technology
Georgia State University
Morehouse College
Southern Polytechnic State University

Ronald E. McNair Elementary, Middle and High Schools

Nationally— Twenty-two (22) including three schools in Metropolitan Atlanta Public School Systems

Dr. Ronald E. McNair Memorial Park, Library & Museum

Lake City, South Carolina

Challenger Learning Centers

NASA

Massachusetts Institute of Technology

North Carolina A&T State University

Spelman College— NASA Women in Science and Engineering Program (W.I.S.E.)

United States Space Foundation

Shortly after the Challenger accident, I received a telephone call from South Carolina's U.S. Senator Strom Thurmond. He graciously expressed condolences to the McNair family.

Over the next few months, several telephone conversations, correspondences and meetings ensued with Senator Thurmond regarding the Dr. Ronald E. McNair Foundation. We shared with him the family's desire to create a living memorial to honor Ron's life and his quest to inspire students to be achievers.

After considerable thought and deliberation, the Senator called to inquirer as to whether the family would approve of a bill that he was planning to introduce to the Senate. His request was met with overwhelming approval.

On April 8, 1987, Senator Thurmond appealed on our behalf, before the United States Senate, a special bill of legislation. This Bill would honor my brother by naming the Post-Baccalaureate Achievement Program under the Higher Education Act of 1965 as the "Ronald E. McNair Post-Baccalaureate Achievement Program." The program is designed to assist and encourage disadvantaged students, who have completed their sophomore year in postsecondary education, to apply for and enroll in graduate programs.

STROM THURMOND
SOUTH CAROLINA
COMMITTEES

ARMED SERVICES
JUDICIARY
VETERANS' AFFAIRS
LABOR AND HUMAN RESOURCES

United States Senate

WASHINGTON, DC 20510

April 8, 1987

Mr. Carl S. McNair, Jr.
2859 Royal Path Court
Becuter, Georgia 30030

Dear Mr. McNair:

Please find enclosed a copy of a bill I introduced April 8, 1987 to honor your late brother, Dr. McNair, by naming the Post-Baccalaureate Achievement Program under the Higher Education Act of 1965 as the "Ronald E. McNair Post-Baccalaureate Achievement Program". I have also enclosed a copy of a statement I delivered upon introduction of this measure.

It was a great pleasure to introduce this legislation. Dr. McNair was certainly an example to us all, and makes a great symbol of achievement for the young people of this Nation.

Anytime I may be of assistance, please do not hesitate to contact me.

With kindest regards and best wishes,

Sincerely,

Strom Thurmond

Strom Thurmond

ST/rzz
Enclosures

Dr. Ronald E. Mcnair
Post-baccalaureate Achievement Programs

———

Schools Named In Honor Of
Dr. Ronald E. Mcnair · Astronaut

———

Photographs

———

RONALD E. MCNAIR POST-BACCALAUREATE ACHIEVEMENT PROGRAMS

ALABAMA
Talladega College
University of Alabama-Birmingham
University of Alabama-Tuscaloosa
University of Montevallo

ARKANSAS
Arkansas State University
Harding University
Henderson State University
University of Arkansas at Little Rock
University of Arkansas-Pine Bluff

ARIZONA
Embry-Riddle Aeronautical
University-Prescott
University of Arizona

CALIFORNIA
California State Polytechnic
University-Pomona
California State University- Fresno
California State University-Bakersfield
California State University-
Dominguez Hills
California State University-Fullerton
California State University-Long Beach
California State University-Sacramento
California State University-
San Bernardino
Claremont Graduate University
San Diego State University
San Jose State University
University of California-Berkeley
University of California-Davis
University of California-Los Angeles
University of California-San Diego
University of San Diego
University of Southern California

COLORADO
Colorado State University
University of Colorado- Denver

University of Colorado-Boulder
University of Northern Colorado

DISTRICT OF COLUMBIA
American University
Howard University

DELAWARE
Delaware State University
University of Delaware

FLORIDA
Florida A&M University
Florida International University
University of Central Florida
University of Florida

GEORGIA
Georgia Southern University
Georgia State University
Morehouse College

HAWAII
Chaminade University of Honolulu

IOWA
Iowa State University
University of Northern Iowa

IDAHO
Boise State University
University of Idaho

ILLINOIS
DePaul University
Governors State University
Knox College
Northeastern Illinois University
Southern Illinois University-Carbondale
University of Chicago
University of Illinois-
Urbana-Champaign
University of Illinois-Chicago

INDIANA
Indiana State University-Terre Haute
Indiana University-Bloomington
Indiana University-Purdue
University-Indianapolis
Purdue University-Calumet
University of Notre Dame

KANSAS
Kansas State University
University of Kansas
Wichita State University

KENTUCKY
Eastern Kentucky University
Murray State University

LOUISIANA
Louisiana State University
Southern University A&M-Baton Rouge
University of Louisiana-Lafayette
Xavier University of Louisiana

MASSACHUSETTS
Boston College
University of Massachusetts-Boston

MARYLAND
Coppin State University
University of Maryland
Baltimore County
University of Maryland-College Park

MICHIGAN
Central Michigan University
Grand Valley State University
Michigan State University
Sienna Heights University
Wayne State University

MINNESOTA
College of St. Scholastica
Minnesota State University-Mankato
University of Minnesota
Central Missouri State University

MISSOURI
Saint Louis University
Southeast Missouri State University

Truman State University
University of Missouri-Columbia

MISSISSIPPI
Jackson State University
University of Mississippi
University of Southern Mississippi

MONTANA
University of Montana

NORTH CAROLINA
Elizabeth City State University
North Carolina A&T State University
University of North
Carolina at Charlotte

NORTH DAKOTA
North Dakota State University
University of North Dakota

NEBRASKA
University of Nebraska-Lincoln
NEW HAMPSHIRE
University of New Hampshire

NEW JERSEY
New Jersey Institute of Technology
Rutgers University

NEW MEXICO
New Mexico State University
University of New Mexico

NEVADA
University of Nevada-Las Vegas
University of Nevada-Reno

NEW YORK
Clarkson University
Columbia University
CUNY-Hunter College
CUNY-John Jay College
CUNY-Lehman College
CUNY-York College
Mercy College
St. John's University
St. Lawrence University
SUNY-Binghamton
SUNY-Brockport
SUNY-Buffalo State College

SUNY-Fredonia
SUNY-Oswego
SUNY-Buffalo
Syracuse University
University of Rochester

OHIO
Kent State University
Oberlin College
Ohio University
University of Akron
University of Cincinnati

OKLAHOMA
Cameron University
East Central University
University of Central Oklahoma
University of Oklahoma

OREGON
Portland State University
Southern Oregon University
University of Oregon

PENNSYLVANIA
Indiana University of Pennsylvania
Pennsylvania State University
Temple University
University of Pennsylvania

PUERTO RICO
Inter-American University of
Puerto Rico-San German
Pontifical Catholic University
of Puerto Rico
University of Puerto Rico-
Humacao Campus

SOUTH CAROLINA
University of South Carolina

TENNESSEE
East Tennessee State University
Fisk University
Middle Tennessee State University
University of Tennessee-Knoxville
University of Tennessee-Memphis

TEXAS
Abilene Christian University
Lamar University
Our Lady of the Lake University
Sam Houston State University
St. Edward's University
Texas A&M University-Kingsville
Texas Christian University
Texas Southern University
Texas Tech University
Texas Woman's University
University of North Texas
University of North Texas Health
Science Center-Fort Worth
University of Texas-Arlington
University of the Incarnate Word
West Texas A&M University

UTAH
Westminster College

VIRGINIA
Virginia Polytechnic Institute
and State University

VERMONT
University of Vermont

WASHINGTON
Eastern Washington University
University of Washington
Washington State University

WISCONSIN
Beloit College
Marquette University
University of Wisconsin-Eau Claire
University of Wisconsin-Madison
University of Wisconsin-Milwaukee
University of Wisconsin-River Falls
University of Wisconsin-Superior
University of Wisconsin-Whitewater

WEST VIRGINIA
Concord University
West Virginia University

WYOMING
University of Wyoming

SCHOOLS NAMED IN HONOR OF
DR. RONALD E. MCNAIR - ASTRONAUT

―――

Ronald E. McNair Elementary	Compton, California
Ronald E. McNair High School	Stockton, California
Ronald E. McNair Elementary	Milwaukee, Wisconsin
Ronald E. McNair Elementary	Denton, Texas
Ronald E. McNair Elementary	Chicago, Illinois
Ronald E. McNair Middle School	College Park, Georgia
Ronald E. McNair Middle School	Decatur, Georgia
Ronald E. McNair High School	Atlanta, Georgia
Ronald E. McNair Middle School	Lake City, South Carolina
Ronald E. McNair Elementary	No. Charleston, South Carolina
Ronald E. McNair Elementary	Fayetteville, Arkansas
Ronald E. McNair School	Detroit, Michigan
Ronald E. McNair Academic High School	Jersey City, New Jersey
PS 5 Ronald E. McNair Elementary	Brooklyn, New York
PS 147 Ronald E. McNair Elementary	Cambria Heights, New York
Ronald E. McNair Elementary	Germantown, Maryland
Ronald E. McNair Sixth Grade	San Antonio, Texas
Ronald E. McNair Elementary	University City, Missouri
Ronald E. McNair Elementary	New Orleans, Louisiana
Ronald E. McNair Magnet Middle School	Cocoa, Florida
Banneker-McNair Math/Science Academy	Houston, Texas
Ronald E. McNair Elementary	Houston, Texas
Ronald E. McNair Elementary	Dallas, Texas
Edison-McNair Academy	East Palo Alto, California

Total   24

PHOTOGRAPHS

Ron with crewmembers of *Challenger* Mission 41-B space flight. (From top left); Robert Stewart , (front)Vance Bland (commander), (front right) Robert "Hoot" Gibson, and Bruce McCandless.

Ronald (holding doll), and Carl, as toddlers.

(We were only 10 months apart.)

Ronald seated at the front of the class at Carver Elementary School.

Sunday morning at grandmother's house (circa 1960).

Dad, (Carl C); Mom, (Pearl); Carl S., Eric (middle)and Ronald.

Maternal Grandfather and Grandmother, James and Mable Montgomery

Dad and the boys off to Sunday morning church service in NY.

Center: Eric
l to r Carl S. , Carl C., and Ronald.

Ron and me sporting the Ray Charles look.

Carver High School lettermen (Left to right: Robert, Ronald, Carl and Ronald (Dirty Red).

Ronald and Carl on Graduation Day, Carver High School.

Freshmen Air force ROTC cadets at NC A&T.

Below: Ron (front, 2nd from left) and fellow Omega Psi Phi
Fraternity pledgees "The Dirty Dozen" at NC A&T.

Ron pictured with William Perry during a Karate session.

Below: The Graduates: Our grandmother, graduated from high school with Eric and Debra (cousin), the same year that Ron and I graduated from college.

Summer break, hanging out with dad at Rockaway Beach, NY
Carl S., Dad and Ron

Brothers and their sweethearts: pictured at a holiday gathering:
l to r Ron and wife Cheryl, and Mary (Carl's wife) and Carl.

228

A scientist in training—Ron conducts experiments at the Massachusetts Institute of Technology (MIT) in the Spectroscopy Laboratory.

Graduation Day at MIT. Pictured are Dr. Ronald E. McNair with his proud parents, Carl C. and Pearl McNair.

Ronald E. McNair, Guion S. Bluford, Jr., Frederick D. Gregory
First African-American Space Shuttle Astronauts

Below: Weightless training aboard the KC-135 jet aircraft ("The Vomit Comet")

Ron and Cheryl
with son, Reggie.

Astronaut training class at Johnson Space Center, Houston, TX.

Lead by Commander Vance Brand, the crewmembers of Space Shuttle Mission 41-B prepare to board Challenger. February 3, 1984

Ronald E. McNair, Mission Specialist aboard the Earth-orbiting Space Shuttle Challenger's Mission 41-B in February 1984, doubles as "director" for an on board movie production; his name tag reads "Cecil B. McNair."

This photo was taken by Ron of crewmember Bruce McCandless
during his exploratory mission 200 ft. away from the Shuttle.

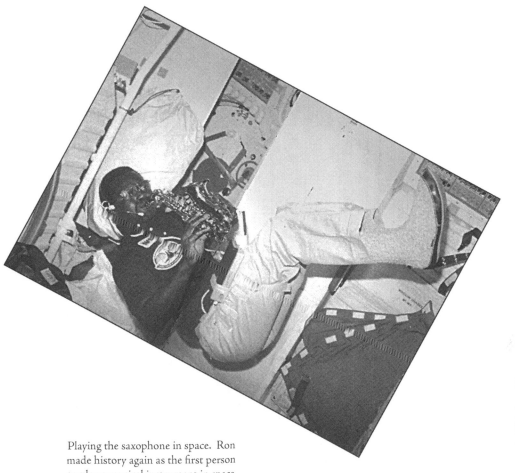

Playing the saxophone in space. Ron made history again as the first person to play a musical instrument in space during the Challenger 41-B flight.

Ron operating space shuttle Remote Manipulator Arm (RMA).

Ron signing autographs after speaking to students at school assembly.

Ron with son, Reggie, at homecoming parade in his honor after his first space flight.

Below, right: Four Generations: Ron with his grandmother, mother and son.

Ron casting his
footprint in cement—
near Lake City
Elementary School,
Lake City, SC.

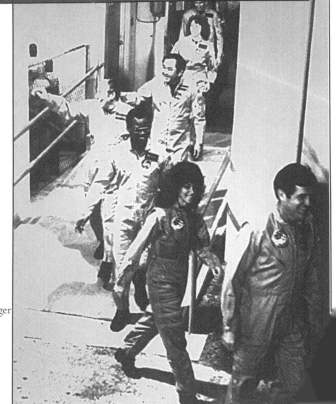

The crew of the Challenger
from l to r

(top)
Ellison S. Onizuka
S. Christa McAuliffe
Gregory B. Jarvis
Judith A. Resnik

(bottom)
Michael J. Smith
Francis R. Scobee
Ronald E. McNair

The crew of Mission 51-L
prepared to board the Challenger
on January 28, 1986.

238

Astronaut Charles F. Bolden, fellow South Carolinian and Ron's close friend, became NASA's liaison to Ron's wife, Cheryl, and the family. He provided assistance and consolation to the family that was deeply appreciated following the *Challenger* accident. Today, Lt. General Bolden is retired from the United States Marine Corps.

Ronald E. McNair Hall— Engineering building at North Carolina A&T State University

The Center For Space Research is located in
The Ronald E. McNair Building at Massachusetts Institute of Technology (MIT)

Dr. Ronald E. McNair
Memorial Park in
Lake City, SC.

Cheryl, with son, Reggie and daughter, Joy, kindles the "eternal flame" during the Dedication of the Mastaba Ceremony (pictured below) at the Dr. Ronald E. McNair Memorial Park, Lake City, SC.

Dr. Ronald E. McNair
Astronaut

Ron and Cheryl with son,
Reggie and daughter, Joy.

Author Carl S. McNair - President of the McNair Achievement Programs, LLC and Founder of the Dr. Ronald E. McNair Foundation - pictured with his lovely wife, Mary and daughter, Desireé.

Ronald E. McNair was a Renaissance man if ever there were one. This book is dedicated to the memory, the hard work, the artistry, and the spirit that will continually be Ron McNair.

Photo Credits
(listed in accordance of appearance)

Courtesy of NASA:
pp. 218, 227-232a, 235, 236a, 239a

Courtesy of McNair Family Archives:
pp. 219-222, 223a, 224b, 225, 226b, 233-234, 236b, 237b, 238b, 239b, 240

Courtesy of Chuck Byrd:
pp. 223b

Courtesy of North Carolina A&T Archives:
pp. 224a

Courtesy of MIT Museum Collection:
pp. 226a, 237a

Courtesy of Lake City News & Post:
pp. 238a

Carl S. McNair, MBA

Carl S. McNair is the President of McNair Achievement Programs, LLC and Founder of the Dr. Ronald E. McNair Foundation. The Foundation is named in honor of his brother who died along with six of his astronaut crewmembers aboard the Space Shuttle Challenger, January 28,1986. Carl is committed to educational programs that inspire and encourage students to pursue careers in Science, Technology, Engineering and/or Mathematics (STEM). Carl has appeared on CNN, ABC, NBC and CBS television networks and featured on the Travis Smiley Show. He lives in Atlanta with his wife, Mary, and daughter, Desiree'.

H. Michael Brewer, Ph.D., is a national award-winning writer who has authored or co-authored five books. He is an adjunct professor at Northern Kentucky University. He and his family reside in Kentucky.

MAP PUBLISHING, LLC
Atlanta, Georgia

We celebrate the Life and Legacy of Dr. Ronald E. McNair through this book and twenty-five years of commitment to excellence, manifested through collaborations and partnerships toward the educational development of America's future leaders.

The blessings have been many:
- Over 5,000 students have participated in the McNair Space and Science Camps since initiated in 1988.
- More than 700 multi-disciplined, public and private school teachers have participated in the Ronald E. McNair Teaching with Space In-Service Training Program.
- More than 50,000 McNair Scholars have participated in the Ronald E. McNair Post-Baccalaureate Achievement Program (US Dept. of Ed.). Over 100 McNair Scholars have earned doctorate degrees.
- Naming of 22 elementary, middle and high schools in honor of Astronaut Dr. Ronald E. McNair.
- Numerous collaborations with the U.S. Department of Education, National Aeronautics and Space Administration (NASA), Massachusetts Institute of Technology (MIT), North Carolina A & T State University, and numerous colleges, businesses, organizations and municipalities.

The U.S. Department of Education annually funds the Ronald E. McNair Post-Baccalaureate Achievement Programs, which awards grants totaling more than $42 million dollars to 201 colleges and universities to prepare students for doctoral studies.